# *Tell the World*

## *Storytelling Across Language Barriers*

Compiled and Edited by Margaret Read MacDonald

**LIBRARIES**

**U N L I M I T E D**

A Member of the Greenwood Publishing Group

Westport, Connecticut • London

Library of Congress Cataloging-in-Publication Data

Tell the world : storytelling across language barriers / compiled and edited by
Margaret Read MacDonald.
    p. cm.
    Includes bibliographical references and index.
    ISBN 978-1-59158-314-1 (alk. paper)
    1. Storytelling.   2. Translating and interpreting.   I. MacDonald, Margaret Read,
1940–
    LB1042.T44 2008
    372.67′7 — dc22        2007022722

British Library Cataloguing in Publication Data is available.

Library of Congress Catalog Card Number: 2007022722
ISBN: 978-1-59158-314-1

First published in 2008

Libraries Unlimited, 88 Post Road West, Westport, CT 06881
A Member of the Greenwood Publishing Group, Inc.
www.lu.com

Printed in the United States of America

The paper used in this book complies with the
Permanent Paper Standard issued by the National
Information Standards Organization (Z39.48–1984).

10   9   8   7   6   5   4   3   2   1

*This book is dedicated to Barb Ittner, editor of
the Libraries Unlimited World Folklore series.
Barb has worked tirelessly over the years to bring us amazing folktales
from around the world. Because of her caring, we can read tales
from the tellers of Australia, Brazil, Cuba, Haiti, India,
Indonesia, Korea, Thailand, and twenty other cultures!*

# Contents

# Introduction

Scene one: It is Sunday afternoon, but the Kiambu school lawn is full of children who have come to hear stories. Sam Mbure invites them here once a month to hear stories told in their own Kikuyu language. The schools teach in Ki-Swahili but Sam wants to nurture their mother tongue. They are speaking Kikuyu and I am speaking English. But this is no barrier. Sam's lively, bilingual daughter is translating my stories for them and their stories for me. She picks up immediately on my line-for-line translation pattern and the stories flow.

Scene two: Several classes of four- and five-year-olds are packed into a room in their preschool in Taoyuan, Taiwan. They laugh and chant along as I tell "Cheese and Crackers," the Kentucky tale of a big old bear who swallows up a little boy. "*Cheesu han bin gun, Cheesu han bin gun*" they holler. Yet they speak only Mandarin and I am telling in English. How can they chant along? Via Jocelyn Chuang, who follows my every move and nuance with her Mandarin equivalent.

Just back from my spring telling tour, I am asked by my editor to write an introduction to this book. I can only reiterate the good advice I have put forth in these pages. Just find yourself a lively bilingual coconspirator and start telling across languages. I had only met Sam Mbure's daughter the moment I stood up to tell. Jocelyn was assigned as my host on a publisher's tour of Taiwan. But I drafted her as co-teller for my workshops and performances, and she jumped into the fray without even time for a rehearsal moment.

The key is a lively compatriot. I shouldn't lead you to believe that this always works right off. In another setting I was assigned a college professor with no sense of pacing and little sense of humor, and she proved an incredible drag on the story. But with a little work and a lot of persistence, you, too, can tell right across those language barriers. And you can help others to do the same.

This book grew from a workshop offered at the 2004 conference of the National Storytelling Network held in Bellingham, Washington. Masako Sueyoshi, Fran Stallings, J. G. Pinkerton, and this author demonstrated and discussed various techniques for translation of storytelling performances.

The hope is that these techniques will be useful not only to tellers who desire to work abroad or in translation at home, but also to those who want to find ways to present tellers who do not speak their language. A search of our immigrant communities often turns up amazing folks who have hearts full of stories to share. But presenting these to audiences who do not understand the teller's language can be a challenge.

In this book you will find reports of the firsthand experiences of tellers who have worked across language barriers. I speak of my own work with translators in Asia and Latin America. Fran Stallings shares her work with the Japanese teller Hiroko Fujita.

Joe Hayes, Ricardo Provencio, Olga Loya, Michael Harvey, Angela Lloyd, and Martin Ellrodt explain how it feels to tell bilingually. Wajuppa Tossa, Livia de Almeida, Paula Martín, and Masako Sueyoshi talk of the translator's role. Masako Sueyoshi, Jill Johnson, Neppe Pettersson, and Priscilla Howe talk of attempting to tell in a language in which they are less than fluent. Murti Bunanta, Kevin Cordi, Ben Haggarty, Regina Ress, Tim Sheppard, and others comment on the problems and pleasures of presenting tellers who speak languages other than those of the audience. Mama Edie Armstrong, Michael Harvey, Cathy Spagnoli, and David Titus talk of the ways culture affects communication. Laura Simms shares a touching word on her own attempts to share with Roma women. Lois Sprengnether Keel and Karee Wardrop speak on sign language translation. Nat Whitman, Julie Klein, Michael Harvey, and Judith Wynhausen tell of using story in educational settings. And Dianne de Las Casas, Cathryn Fairlee, Michael Harvey, Bob Kanegis, Mary Grace Ketner, Caren S. Neile, Regina Ress, Cathy Spagnoli, and Ruth Stotter share tips from their own experiences telling in cultures other than their own.

A bibliography is provided citing numerous folktale collections that have been translated into other languages. Hopefully some of these can aid in preparing texts for your own telling abroad.

I thank the thirty-nine tellers who have so eagerly contributed anecdotes and tips that may help future tellers on their own storytelling road. These are only a few of the many tellers who are traveling the globe . . . moving from country to country . . . sharing tales. It is in just this way that folktales have been passed around and around the world for centuries. So readers, please join them! Pack up your stories . . . use the tips from the tellers in this book to help you imagine your own sharing across languages . . . and take to the road! We hope these reports of our own trials and errors help.

And don't fail to invite in the teller down the street in your own town, who just happens to speak a different language. Use these techniques to present tellers to your own audiences. Through our stories we can build bridges of friendship. Don't let language be a barrier!

# Chapter 2

# Line-by-Line Translation

## Margaret Read MacDonald

A useful technique that can be used for storytelling or for public speaking is line-by-line translation. At first one might expect this to be a rather clunky delivery . . . stop . . . start . . . stop . . . start. . . . But in fact this can be a very fluid process.

The key to creating an easy flow of language in line-by-line translation is in the pacing. The speaker/teller needs to pause frequently to allow the translation to keep pace. Yet the pauses must be at natural speech pauses. And rather than dropping the voice in an attitude of "now I will pause for the translation," the teller should hold both gesture and tone as if simply pausing in speech. When working in this format, I sometimes even vocally hold the last vowel, letting the translator begin speaking over my last word. The teller and translator move along rapidly together in an easy dance of language.

For example, here is the beginning of "The Squeaky Door/*La puerta que chilla*" as Paula Martín and I would do it.

Once upon a time
*Habia una vez*
Little boy went to his Grandma's house to spend the night.
*Un niño fue a dormir a la casa de su abuela.*
"I have a surprise for you! You get to sleep in the big brass bed . . . all by
   yourself!"
"*¡Tengo una sorpresa para tí! "¡Dormirás en la cama grande de bronce*
   *. . . tú solito!*
*¿Vas a tener miedo?*"
"Are you going to be scared?"
And the little boy said: "No! Not ME!"
*El niño dijo: "¿Yo? ¡NO!*"

The next time we reach this part of the story, we will move rapidly through the translation and encourage the audience to repeat *both languages* with us.

*"¿Vas a tener miedo?"*

Audience responds: *"No! Not ME! ¡Yo . . . NO!"* In stories such as this that use much repetition, the translation can move rapidly as the audience begins to anticipate what is coming.

In line-by-line translation that has been rehearsed with another teller, the translating teller can take the lead at times, as Paula does above in the line *"¿Vas a tener miedo?"* The tale appears in a picture book: *The Squeaky Door* by Margaret Read MacDonald, illus. by Mary Newell DePalma [HarperCollins, 2006], and in *A Parent's Guide to Storytelling* [August House, 1995], and its translations, *Quentos que van y vienen*, trans. Paula Martín [Aique, 2001] and *Kattate Ageteyo!*, trans. Ryoko Sato [Amu Shobu, 2002]. A picture book version is also available in the Korean language from Gipun Publishers.)

The line-by-line translation method requires that the teller examine his or her material with an eye to where pauses should be made for best effect. Once the teller has perfected a delivery that allows breaks for translation, any translator can be used. Performances work best if a translator can be found who is also a storyteller. But a perfectly adequate performance can be presented using any bilingual individual who agrees to translate.

Rehearsal is important, but not always possible. Even a short rehearsal time will give your translator an idea of your speech mode and an ear for your voice. Always rehearse in the posture in which you will be telling. If you will be standing, stand. If you will be sitting, sit. Use gestures as you rehearse, and tell in your full performance mode. Some translators will pick up on your gestures and intonation and begin to "tandem tell" with you. For the most effective presentation the story should be delivered as if two tellers are standing side-by-side delivering the same story . . . just in different languages. Both are telling.

Even if the rehearsal period is brief, go through at least one story from beginning to end with all performative parts. Clue the translator in about the entire program, and quickly discuss any problems they might encounter, such as unusual words or concepts the translator might not understand. Once in Thailand I was telling Vi Hilbert's Lushootseed story of the chiefs who tell their people to push up the sky. Halfway through the story, my translator, Wajuppa suddenly stopped and looked at me in alarm: "Are you saying *Chiefs*? I thought you were saying *Sheep*!" She told the audience to never mind about the "sheep pushing up the sky." It was *chiefs* all along. They laughed and we continued. The story probably would have worked even if they had misunderstood it. For, as in many stories, it is the action that counts.

When my daughter was young, her favorite story was Joseph Jacobs's tale of "Mr. Fox." In the story Lady Mary approaches the castle of the wicked Mr. Fox and sees signs over the gates that read, "Be bold, be bold . . . but not *too* bold . . . ." Julie had heard this story every Halloween from her Brownie Scout years on. Long about age twelve, she suddenly sat up straight and stared. "Mom! You are saying, "Be bold . . . be bold . . . ." I always thought you were saying, "Be bald . . . be bald . . . but not *too* bald."

The story had made perfect sense to her even with this slight linguistic gap. And it is thus with our storytelling in other languages. Likely certain phrases and words are misunderstood or lost in translation. But the overwhelming joy . . . the rush of the story . . . carries on. And if our story is told in Thailand as one of sheep lifting the sky? Well, why not!

So I advise those who end up in settings in which they don't quite speak the local language . . . .just be bold . . . be bold . . . go ahead, and be *very* bold!

*Chapter 3*

# Tandem Telling

For me, the most enjoyable translation technique is through tandem telling with another storyteller/translator. With this method, the two of you tell side-by-side as one performance. The sense of a "translator" is replaced by that of a second teller. This requires practice . . . perhaps hours of practice. Timing is everything. And many artistic decisions need to be made about style of presentation.

Tandem telling can be done simply, in the line-by-line style discussed in the previous chapter. But working in Japan with Masako Sueyoshi, the two of us developed variations to this form, which prove fun onstage.

## TANDEM-TELLING TECHNIQUES

### Audience Contact

Both Masako and I relate to the audience . . . making eye contact with the listeners . . . and encouraging audience participation. Though we may be assuming roles within the stories, we may break role temporarily to help get the audience chanting or singing along. So we both are acting as lead teller in this sense. Both are assuming responsibility for working the audience. Though I speak first (in English), we both are telling the story.

### Acting Out

This technique works especially well with stories that have only two characters. Each teller can assume the role of one character. We include a transcript of our telling of "Grandfather Bear Is Hungry" below. It includes techniques of side-by-side telling, acting out the tale, dropping translation for repeated phrases, speaking over the other teller's voice, and using a "replay" technique.

When telling the story of "Grandfather Bear Is Hungry," Masako assumes the role of the chipmunk and I that of the bear. While I tell the first part of the story, I move as Bear and Masako remains still while translating. Then she assumes the role of Chipmunk and simply acts out her part in Japanese, while I continue to act the part of Bear in English. Because the story has repetition, the audience by now understands my English repeated phrase "I am so hungry!" So no translation for the bear is needed.

When working with your stories in translation, watch for those spots where translation might no longer be needed. Once the audience has been exposed to an English phrase several times, you can often drop the translation and move the story along more rapidly.

In the telling that follows, either teller or both tellers can be encouraging the audience participation. Here is the story as we perform it.

---

### GRANDFATHER BEAR IS HUNGRY

English-Japanese Telling

by Margaret Read MacDonald and Masako Sueyoshi

This tale is retold from "Grandfather Bear Is Hungry" in *Look Back and See: Twenty Lively Tales for Gentle Tellers* (H. W. Wilson, 1991).

MRM:   Grandfather Bear woke up one fine spring morning.
MS:   *Aru hareta haru no asa , kuma-jiisan wa me wo samashimashita.*
MRM:   He came out of his cave. [Stretching]
    He had been sleeping all winter.
    He was SOOOO hungry.
MS:   *Kuma-jiisan ga hora-ana kara detekimashita.*
    *Fuyu no aida zutto nemutte itanodesu.*
    *Kuma-jiisan wa onaka ga peko-peko deshita.*

MRM:   I am SOOOO hungry. I am SOOO hungry.
MS:   *Aaaaa harapeko daaaaa.*
MRM:   Grandfather Bear thought he would have berries for breakfast.
    He went to the berry patch. [Acting berry search]
MS:   *Kuma-jiisan wa asa-gohan ni ichigo wo tabeyo to omoimashita.*
    *Sokode, ichigo no shigemi ni itte mimashita.*
MRM:   No berries! It was too early in the spring!
MS:   *Ichigo nante natte imasen! Haru wa mada hayasugita no desu.*
MRM:   I am SOOOO hungry!
    I am SOOO hungry!
MS:   *Aaaaa harapeko daaaaa.*

[Coming in on MRM's second line so that we overlap] [Acting and encouraging audience to participate]

MRM:   Grandfather Bear thought he would have a salmon for his breakfast.
       He went down to the stream. [Acting the search]
MS:    *Kuma-jiisan wa asa-gohan ni sake wo tabeyo to omoimashita.*
       *Sokode, ogawa ni itte mimashita.*
MRM:   No salmon! Too early in the spring!
MS:    *Sake nante oyoide imasen! Haru wa mada hayasugita no desu.*
MRM:   I am Sooo hungry! I am SOOOO hungry! [Acting]
MS:    [Simultaneously] [Acting and encouraging audience to participate]
       *Aaaaa harapeko daaaaa.*
MRM:   Grandfather Bear went to the rotten stump.
       He thought he would have bugs and grubs for his breakfast.
MS:    *Kuma-jiisan wa kusatta kirikabu no tokoro ni ikimashita.*
       *Asa-gohan ni mushi wo tabeyo to omotta no desu.*
MRM:   That stump was the home of Little Chipmunk!

[Masako does not use the word for *Chipmunk* in her text . . . because the Japanese word for *Chipmunk* means "striped squirrel." So she just calls him "Little Squirrel" until the last line of the story.]

MS:    *Sono kirikabu wa chiisana risu no ie deshita.*

[MS squats down and pretends to be in stump, acting part of chipmunk]

MS:    *Uwaaaaaaaaaaaaaaa.*
MRM:   He began to rake and scrape at the stump. [MRM pretending to
       rake at stump, while MS feels the shaking]
MS:    *Ojiisan, Ojiisan, nani wo shiteiruno?*
       [Grandfather Bear! Grandfather Bear! What are you doing?]
MRM:   I am SOOOO hungry. I am SOoooo hungry.
MS:    *E? Onaka ga pekopeko nano? Soreja, boku ga tabemono wo wakete*
       *ageruyo. Boku no uchi ni tameteoita donguri ya hoshi-ichigo ga arunda.*
       *Chotto mattetene.*
       [You are hungry? I will share with you. I saved food in my home. Wait
       a minute.]
MRM:   You have acorns and dried berries? I will wait!
MS:    [Brings up food] *Doozo.* [Here you are.]
MRM:   Thank you, Chipmunk! But I am STILL HUNGRY! I am STILL
       HUNGRY! [Encouraging audience to participate]

MS:    *Chyotto mattetene.* [Wait a minute.]

[Acting, brings up more] *Doozo.*

MRM:   Thank you, Chipmunk! But I am STILL HUNGRY! I am STILL
       HUNGRY! [Encouraging audience to participate]

MS:   (Acting) *Chyotto mattetene*. [Wait a minute.]

[Acting, brings up more] *Doozo.*

MRM:   Thank you, Chipmunk! But I am STILL HUNGRY! I am STILL
      HUNGRY! [Encouraging audience to participate]

MS:   Wait a minute. [Acting] *Chyotto mattetene.*
      [Acting, brings up more] *Doozo.*

[Runs up and down, up and down, bringing more and more]

MRM:   [Eats and eats] Hungry! Still Hungry! Still hungry!

[MRM pretends to be full then changes mind . . . . ] Still hungry!

MS:   [Exhausted] *Doozo.* [Here.]

MRM:   At last Grandfather Bear was full.

MS:   *Onaka ippai ni natta?* [You are full?]

MRM:   I want to give you a reward.
      Hold very still.

MS:   *E? Nanika gohobi wo kureruno?* [You want to give me a reward?]

MRM:   Very gently Grandfather Bear pulled his heavy claw down chip-
      munk's back. He left five black stripes.

MS:   *Kuma-jiisan wa risu no senaka wo tsume de yasashiku sotto nadeoros-
      himashita. Suruto, risu no senaka ni gōhon no shima-moyo ga dekimas-
      hita.*

MRM:   Now when anyone sees you they will see your stripes.
      They will remember how kind you were to share with Grandfather
      Bear.

MS:   *Korekara wa mina ga omae no shima-moyo wo miru tabini,
      omae ga washi ni tabemono wo wakete kureta shinsetsu wo omoidasu
      daroyo.*

[Masako now gives a final sentence explaining that Chipmunk, since then,
has five beautiful stripes. This is the first time she has used the Japanese
word for *Chipmunk* . . . because *Shima-risu* means "striped squirrel"; that
is, shima = squirrel and risu = striped.] *Shima-risu no senaka ni utsukusii
gôhon no shima-moyo ga dekitanowa konotoki kara nanodesuyo.*

---

## Dropping Translation for Words and Phrases

When working with your stories in translation, watch for spots where translation might no longer be needed at all. Once the audience has been exposed to an English phrase several times, you can often drop the translation
and move the story along faster.

In "Grandfather Bear Is Hungry," we do not need to translate Grandfather Bear's cry, "I am sooo hungry!" more than a time or two. As soon as
the audience is chiming in with us, Masako can stop translating that phrase.

Toward the end of the story she is acting Chipmunk's part out in Japanese and I am simply repeating the phrase, which is now well understood. This allows her to drop the role of translator altogether for a time.

## Voice-Over

We move the story along more quickly and create a seamless telling by sometimes speaking at the same time. Masako chimes in with her translation before I have finished my phrase. Or at times I will hold the final vowel sound in a word until her translation has begun . . . giving the performance a knitted together feel.

An example of this appears in "Grandfather Bear Is Hungry." On the second reiteration of the bear's cry, "I am SOOO Hungry," Masako begins her Japanese translation during my second repetition. By the third repetition, we are speaking simultaneously and acting out the hungry bear together . . . one in English . . . the other in Japanese.

## Replay

A useful tandem technique we have developed is that of repeating what the other person said conversationally, rather than as translation. For example, in the story of Grandfather Bear, the bear says, "I want to give you a reward." The chipmunk replies in Japanese, "You want to give me a reward?" Translation of Grandfather Bear's line is thus not needed.

There are many ways this "replay" can be phrased. Some examples follow from another story:

Little Boy Snake says: "Teach me how to hop."
Little Boy Frog replies in Japanese: "You say you want me to teach you how to hop?"

Or: "You want me to teach you how to hop?"
Or: "Yes, I could teach you how to hop."
Or: "If you want to learn how to hop, try this . . . "
Or: "Try this . . . " [Demonstrating]

The amount of information you need to translate verbally will depend on how much you both are conveying via body language.

The replay technique is used extensively in our retelling of "Little Boy Frog and Little Boy Snake" below. Use of this method allows us to move the story along much more quickly than we could do with line-by-line translation.

## English Phrases Stressed for English Language Learning

In the tale of "Little Boy Frog and Little Boy Snake," we also eliminate translation time by choosing to both say a few phrases together in English: "hop hop hop" and "slide slide slide." If we were simply trying to communicate the story to a Japanese audience, we might also use this technique with some Japanese phrases. But one side effect that teachers expect from our telling is an exposure to spoken English. So we lean toward more use of English.

The idea is to move the story along as swiftly as possible but without losing any of the fun English language repetition.

Here is our dual text for "Little Boy Frog and Little Boy Snake."

---

## LITTLE BOY FROG AND LITTLE BOY SNAKE

English-Japanese Telling

by Margaret Read MacDonald and Masako Sueyoshi

This tale is retold from "Little Boy Frog and Little Boy Snake" in *Shake-it-Up Tales: Stories to Sing, Dance, Drum and Act-Out* (August House, 2000).

MRM:   Little Boy Snake woke up one morning.

MS:   *Aru asa Hebi-kun ga me wo samashimashita*

MRM:   He said, "Mama! Mama! I want to go up the mountain to play! [Entering the role of Little Boy Snake and addressing Masako as if she is his mother]

MS:   *Oya, yama ni asobi ni ikitaino?* [You want to go up the mountain to play?] *Soreja, ki wo tsukete itte rassyai. Shiranai hito to osyaberi shitewa ikemasenyo. Sorekara, kurakunaru maeni kaette irassyai.* [Well, be careful where you go. Don't talk to strangers. And get home before dark.]

MRM:   All right. I'll be careful where I go. I won't talk to strangers. I'll come home before dark. [To mother]
So Little Boy Snake went up the mountain. [To audience as narrator] [Acting] Slide slide slide . . . [As Little Boy Snake]

MS:   *Sokode Hebi-kun wa yama ni nobotte ikimashita.*
*Nyoro nyoro nyoro . . .*

MRM:   [Gesturing to Masako] On the other side of the mountain Little Boy Frog woke up.

MS:   *Sate, yama no hantaigawa dewa Kaeru-kun ga me wo samashima-shita.*

MS:   [Addressing MRM as if MRM is his mother]
      *Kaachan kaachan! Yama ni ikitaiyo.* [Mama! Mama! I want to go up
      the mountain!]
MRM:   You want to go up the mountain? Well, be careful where you go.
      Don't talk to strangers. And come home before dark.
MS:   *Un, kiwotsukete itte kuruyo. Shiranai hito towa osyaberi shinaiyo. Kur-
      aku naru maeni kaette kuruyo.* [I'll be careful where I go. I won't talk
      to strangers. I'll come home before dark.]
MRM:   So Little Boy Frog went up the mountain.
MS:   *Sokode, Kaeru-kun mo yama ni nobotte ikimashita.*
      *Pyon . . . pyon . . . pyon.*
MRM:   Little Boy Snake and Little Boy Frog met on top of the mountain.
MS:   *Hebi-kun to Kaeru-kun wa yama no teppen de aimashita.*
MRM:   Who are you? And what are you doing?
MS:   *Kimi wa dare? Nani wo shite iruno?* [Who are YOU! What are YOU
      doing?]
MRM:   I am Little Boy Frog.
MS:   *Kaeru-kun? Boku wa Hebi-kun dayo.* [Little Boy Frog? I am Little
      Boy Snake.]
MRM:   You are Little Boy Snake?
      What were you doing?
MS:   *Boku jimen wo hatte irundayo. Kimi koso nani wo shiteitano?* [I am
      sliding. What were YOU doing?]
MRM:   You were sliding? I was hopping!
MS:   *Tobihanete itano? Ne-e, boku nimo oshieteyo?* [You were hopping?
      Can you teach me how to hop?]
MRM:   You want to learn how to hop?
      OK. You have to gather all your muscles and JUMP into the air. Like
      this! [Demonstrates]
MS:   *Zenshin no kinniku wo tsukatte . . . Kuuchu ni tobihanerundane? . . .
      nyooooo!* [Trying it]
      [Gather all my muscles . . . JUMP into the air!]
MRM: No higher. Like this!
MS:   *Yatte miruyo. nyoooo-ron!* [Trying to jump]
      *Muzukashii-ya! Demo, omoshiroi!*
      [I'll try again. Jump! It's hard! But it's fun!]
      *Isho-ni tobihaneyo!* [Let's play hop!]
MRM:   OK. Let's play hop!

[The two hop around the stage . . . frog doing well, snake barely getting off
the ground]

MRM:   Hop hop hop hop
MS:   [In English] Hop hop hop hop
      *Nyooooo-ron! Nyoooo-ron!*

MS:  [Laughing] Aa *omoshirokatta*! [That was fun!]

MRM:  Now you teach ME how to SLIDE.

MS:  *E? kimi jimen no haikata wo oboetaino?* [You want to learn how to slide?]

MRM:  Yes. You teach me.

MS:  *Jimen ni petari-to haitsukubatte. . . .* [You have to lie flat on the ground].

MRM:  Lie flat on the ground?

MS:  *Un sodayo. Soshite mae ni susumundayo.* [Yes. Now slide forward.]

MRM:  Slide forward. Like this? [Tries]

MS:  *Mo-ichido yatte gorann-yo.* [No. Try it again.]

MRM:  Slide. Slide. Slide. It tickles my tummy.

MS:  *E? onaka ga kusuguttai-no? Gannbatte.* [It tickles your tummy? Well, keep trying.]

MRM:  Let's play Slide!

MS and MRM:  Slide Slide Slide Slide [Sliding around the stage, both speaking English]

  *Nyoo-ron nyoo-ron nyoo-ron . . .*

MRM:  That was fun!

MS:  *Un, omoshirokatta-ne.* [Wasn't that fun?]

MRM:  Oh, oh. It's getting dark. We'd better go home.

MS:  *Kuraku natte kita. Ouchi ni kaero.* [Getting dark. Let's go home.]

MRM:  Can you come play tomorrow?

MS:  *Ashita mo asoberukatte? Mochironndayo.* [Come play tomorrow? Yes.]

MRM:  Say . . . are you my new friend?

MS:  *Kimi, boku no otomodachi?* [Are you my friend?]

MRM:  Yes . . . FRIENDS!

MS:  *Tomodachi!* [Friends!]

MRM:  Goodbye, friend.

MS:  *Sayonara, tomodachi.* [Goodbye, friend.]

MRM:  And Little Boy Frog went down the mountain.

MS:  *Kaeru-kun wa yama wo orite ikimashita.*

  Hop hop hop hop . . . slide slide slide slide . . . hop hop hop hop [Acting]

  *Pyon-rori, pyon-rori, pyon-rori . . .*

MS:  *Hebi-kun wa yama wo orite ikimashita.* [Little Boy Snake went down the mountain.]

  [In English] Slide slide slide slide. . . . hop hop hop hop . . . slide slide slide slide . . . [Acting]

  *Nyo-ron, nyo-ron, nyo-ron*

MRM:  Little Boy Frog's Momma saw him coming.

MS:  *Kaeru-kun no kaatyan wa kaeru-kun ga yattekurunowo mimashita.*

MS:  *Naniwo shite irundai?* [WHAT are you doing?]

MRM:   What am I doing? I am sliding!

MS:   *Jimen wo hatte iru-tte? Darega sonnakoto wo oshietano?* [You are SLIDING? Who taught you to do that?]

MRM:   My new friend.

MS:   *Atarashii tomodachi? Sonoko no namae wa?* [Your new friend? What is his name?]

MRM:   His name is Little Boy Snake.

MS:   *Hebi?!*
*Hebi nannkato asonnja damedayo!*
*Hebi wa watashi-ra no teki nanndakara-ne.*
[Little Boy SNAKE! You can't play with SNAKES.
SNAKES are our ENEMIES!]

MRM:   Snakes are our enemies? I didn't know.

[Pause]

MRM:   Meanwhile on the other side of the mountain Little Boy Snake was going home.

MS:   *Sonoaidani , Hebi-kun ga yama no hanntaigawa wo orite ikimashita.*
[On the other side of the mountain Little Boy Snake was going home.]
[In English] Slide . . . slide . . . slide . . . hop . . . hop . . . hop . . . slide . . . slide . . . slide . . .
*Nyo-ron . . . nyo-ron . . . nyo-ron . . .*

[Note that this is a direct repeat of the previous action. So less translation is necessary.]

MRM:   WHAT are you doing? (Assuming role of Snake Mother)

MS:   *Boku tobihanete irundayo.* [I am hopping.]

MRM:   Hopping? WHO taught you to do that?

MS:   *Boku no atarashii otomodachi ga oshiete kuretanndayo.* [My new friend taught me.]

MRM:   What is your new friend's name?

MS:   *Atarashii otomodachi no namae wa Kaeru-kun te iundayo.* [My new friend's name is Little Boy Frog.]

MRM:   FROG! You can't play with frogs! Frogs are not our friends!

MS:   *Kaeru wa nakama ja naino? Shiranakattayo . . .* [Frogs are not our friends . . . I didn't know.]

[Pause]

MRM:   Next day Little Boy Frog went up the mountain.
Hop . . . hop . . . hop . . . hop . . .

MS:   *Tsugi no hi Hebi-kun mo yama ni nobotte ikimashita.*
[Next day Little Boy Snake went up the mountain]
[English] Slide . . . slide . . . slide . . . slide . . .

MRM:   I can't play with you anymore. Snakes are our enemies.

MS:   *Boku mo kimi towa mou asobenainnda. Kaeru wa nakama ja nain-datte.*

I can't play with you anymore either. Frogs are not our friends.

MRM:   Bye bye.

MS:   *Sayonara.*

MRM:   But wait. Watch what I can do!

MS:   *E? nani ga dekirutte?* [Watch what you can do?]

MRM:   Yes. Slide . . . slide . . . slide . . . slide . . .

MS:   *Boku modayo! Miteyo!* [ME too! Watch what I can do!]

[English] Hop . . . hop . . . hop . . . hop . . .

*Nyo-ron . . . nyo-ron . . . nyo-ron . . .*

MRM:   Bye bye, Friend.

MS:   *Sayonara, tomodachi.*

MRM:   So Little Boy Frog went down the mountain . . . . Hop hop hop hop . . . slide slide slide slide

MS:   *Hebi-kun wa yama wo orite ikimashita.* [And Little Boy Snake went down the mountain.]

[English]    Slide . . . slide . . . slide . . . slide . . . .hop . . . .hop . . . hop . . . hop . . .

*Nyo-ron, nyo-ron, nyo-ron . . .*

MRM:   They couldn't play together anymore.

But they could still be friends.

MS:   *Futari wa nidoto issyoni asobukotowa nakatta keredo zutto tomodachi deshita.*

[They couldn't play together anymore. But they could still be friends.]

---

We hope these sample tales show possibilities for tandem telling. Find a bilingual teller and set aside a good period of time to rehearse. The easy flow between teller and teller requires practice. Masako and I work over these tales again and again . . . looking for ways to smooth out the tellings and move them along more rapidly. We try various techniques until we hit on the one that seems to work well to convey this particular tale to our audiences.

# Chapter 4

# More Than Words:
# Storytelling Without Translation

## Fran Stallings

*Fran Stallings (Oklahoma) and Hiroko Fujita (Japan) have been tell-
ing stories together in each other's countries since 1995. Fran provides introductory synopses in English when Fujita-san tells her traditional tales in Japanese to American audiences. When Fran tells
in Japan, Fujita-san gives Japanese synopses. In 2003 they received
the International Storybridge award from the National Storytelling
Network for their work on both sides of the Pacific.*

### PRESENTING HIROKO FUJITA

When a story depends on clever dialogue, vivid description, and other verbal flourishes, we need an excellent translation in order to savor every word.
But there is more to storytelling than words.

Psycholinguist Suzette Haden Elgin told me that face-to-face communication is like a song and dance performance. The words provide the lyrics,
an expressive voice adds melody, and the gestures and facial expressions do
the dance. A printed story provides only the words. Skilled tellers bring the
story to life by adding the melody and the dance. Storytelling styles differ
in how much "melody" and "dance" particular tellers add.

When I first encountered the lively folk-style telling of Hiroko Fujita in
Japan in 1993, I could understand only a few words of Japanese—but the
STORY came through clearly, thanks to her voice and actions. I could
catch a few words but found that while I was racking my brain to translate
the "lyrics," I was missing the melody and the dance. I found such delight
when I concentrated on the experience as a whole that I became convinced

that Americans could and would enjoy her telling even if they knew not one word of Japanese.

Searching for the most effective way to present her telling to Americans, I decided against line-for-line translation because I did not want interruptions to distract our listeners from the full experience of her style—and I was sure they could understand her, if we set things up right. I had seen some excellent solo bilingual tellers, and some skilled tandem tellers alternating lines in their two languages. However, I had found that after a few minutes I tended to focus on the English and tune out the foreign teller, and I didn't want folks to do that to Fujita-san.

Recalling the way that opera program notes explain the action of each act so that the audience can concentrate on the high art of the singer/actors, I prepared a short synopsis for each of her tales. In the introduction to each one, I tried hard not to steal her thunder by "telling" it myself. But I did mimic a few of her gestures, to foreshadow key points in the story. I even omitted the endings: "And you will see what happened. . . . " It worked!

"I didn't understand a word she said—but I understood the STORY!"

We have heard this from audience members of all ages in twenty U.S. states. When Fujita-san brought me to Japan to tell my stories in English to children and adults, introducing each with a Japanese synopsis, people spontaneously said the same thing (in Japanese, of course). The melody and the dance can communicate so effectively that our audiences follow the meaning of the story and enjoy it—even when they don't understand a word of the lyrics.

Americans are delighted at their success in understanding and enjoying a foreign culture that they had thought was alien and difficult. Japanese adults often feel embarrassed at their lack of proficiency in the English that they had studied in middle school and high school but seldom use. (As a parallel example: How's your algebra?) Both groups feel very differently after an hour of our stories!

The technique we developed can help you showcase foreign or immigrant tellers who must perform in their native language because their English is not fluent. It enables bilingual students to present the tales of their elders to English-speaking classmates. And if you have a chance to travel overseas but lack time to rehearse a detailed translation or tandem performance with a native teller, you can share many of your stories by preceding each with a synopsis related by your interpreter.

## WHAT WORKS

By trial and error in eleven American tours and five in Japan, we have learned ways to select and present stories in the teller's native language without translation.

## Introductions

Someone fluent in the audience's language must introduce each story with a brief synopsis that outlines the plot but does not give away the ending. Mimicking a few of the teller's gestures provides landmarks that reassure the audience that they are keeping pace. The hard part is to refrain from actually telling the story!

## Plot

The story's plot must be straightforward and simple enough so that the outline in the synopsis is easy to recall. We have found that formula tales work well. These have repeated patterns, such as asking the same question to a series of people or overcoming a series of parallel obstacles. When an episode is followed by another of a very different type, however, it's usually necessary to provide an additional synopsis. We don't like this interruption of the flow.

When I'm telling in Japan, Fujita-san sometimes takes an ongoing role in the story. She speaks her part in Japanese, providing information that keeps the audience with us (and lets us start with a *very* short synopsis of just the initial situation). We have not felt the need for this tandem style in America, however, perhaps because her visual aids (see below) convey so much information.

The plot must not depend on twists of dialogue, verbal conflicts, a clever punch line, or other strictly verbal elements. (However, see the Puns and Word Play section.) The best stories have lots of action that can be illustrated with gestures and facial expressions.

## Simple Language

Language must be simple if some listeners DO know some of the foreign tongue. Fujita-san loves the deep country dialect of Fukushima Prefecture, in which she first heard her stories. But when Japanese-Americans, resident expatriates, or students of Japanese are in our audiences, she tries to use the standard pronunciation she learned at Tokyo Women's University. Old-fashioned words and phrases bring a nostalgic tear to the eye of elderly Japanese-American listeners, but even in Japan Fujita-san avoids archaic words when telling to youngsters.

## Consistent Language

Language must be consistent. English is rich with alternate word choices, and we storytellers pride ourselves on not repeating the same noun or adjective. But all those vocabulary words just make trouble for listeners who may be trying to follow in the teller's language. So if the old man is "grandpa" the first time I mention him, I try not to use "grandfather" or "husband" later.

## Style

Most important: the teller must "sing and dance." Varying the voice to distinguish different characters lets the audience know who's talking. An expressive voice tells whether characters are happy, scared, or sad, and facial expressions reinforce this in a visual language that anthropologists find to be universal. (A boy told Fujita-san, "Fran-san doesn't have puppets but she uses every muscle in her face!") Hand gestures that mime story action help the audience know what's happening. Changes in posture can contribute to characterization and mood. If a lot of space is available and the teller is comfortable moving through the story scene, all the better. Reticent Japanese adults were a bit taken aback by the full-body action I added to some stories. ("*Baka gaijin*," crazy foreigner, was a title I decided to accept gladly.) But nobody missed the meaning of the story. When Fujita-san tells in Japan and when I tell in America, where we can rely on words to convey more of the meaning, our styles are not quite so "*baka*"! But fortunately both of us grew up having to hold the attention of restless younger siblings who trained us to make our tales as lively as possible.

## Visual Aids

Visual aids help too. In her decades of work as a preschool teacher, Fujita-san mastered the use of puppets, props, pictures, and other visual aids to help young native language learners follow her ancient stories. City children were often unfamiliar with the traditional animal characters, farm tools, farmhouse layout, and other information fundamental to the old folktales she wanted to tell. The visual aids that she prepared for them prove extremely helpful for American audiences, too.

I was not accustomed to using puppets or props, but I did collect a few items to bring along in Japan. An inflatable stuffed turkey helps us to introduce a draw and tell story, which I can do when a whiteboard is available. A wooden frog noisemaker plays a part in some of my frog stories. A mouse finger puppet has overcome the shyness of hundreds of small Japanese children whose parents want them to say "harrow" to the foreign storyteller after a performance. Eager to pet the equally shy mouse, they forget to be afraid of the huge weird lady who is holding it.

## Music

Music enhances most stories and provides an easy way for the audience to participate. It's amazing how readily listeners (the younger the better) learn to sing along with a chant or refrain in a foreign tongue. In Fujita-san's "Burglar Baby-sitter" story, after the audience has participated in a long cumulative series of silly baby games of the peek-a-boo type, she sings a traditional lullaby. I am certain that none of the American children have heard it before, but they sing along with her—just a split second behind on every note. Awesome.

I use an Autoharp to accompany repeated refrains in many of the stories I tell in Japan, inviting listeners to join in. However, the favorite tale of Japanese adults is "Shingebiss and the North Wind," which has a continual music background from beginning to end. I fear that few can follow it in any detail because I am unable move or gesture while telling. Yet the audience loves the sound and seems to absorb at least the mood of the story.

## Puns and Word Play

Japanese folktales are full of puns and word play. Although I had feared it would be difficult to share this humor with American audiences, it's been a pleasant surprise to find that even elementary students avidly appreciate it—when we lay the groundwork carefully. The following examples may help you find a way to introduce your foreign language partner's wordplay tales.

1. *Niau.* Japanese cats say "*niau*" instead of "meow." The word also means "It is suitable." Young listeners learn the cat's cry in a funny children's song that also teaches the sounds made by Japanese pig, fox, and *tanuki*. Older listeners can learn it in a version of "The Most Powerful Name" wherein the pet cat meows to accept each name change. Then we are ready to tell about a poor man whose courtship of a rich girl was denied by her father as *un*suitable: "*Niau ja nai!*" Father reluctantly agreed, however, that he would allow the marriage if they could get even one member of the family to approve. We ask listeners to help Fujita-san thunder the disapproval of the grandparents, uncles, brothers, and so on, in turn. "*Niau ja nai!*" At last, the girl brought the family cat into the room. It rubbed against Father's knees and said, "*Niau!*"

2. *Fufu Patapata.* Before giving the story synopsis, I explain about toasting *mochi* snacks in the ashes of the hearth. Melted and gooey inside, crispy outside, they resemble toasted marshmallows in texture—but you have to cool them by blowing (*fu, fu*) and you must brush off the ashes (*pata, pata*).

The story concerns two hungry apprentices who knew their master was toasting *mochi* alone in his room because they heard him blowing and brushing. They didn't dare enter to get a share, however, because they were forbidden to come in unless he called them by name. So the next morning, they told him they had decided to change their names to *Fufu* and *Patapata*. The audience enjoys the silliness of these names as he calls them to sweep, scrub, and the like: *"Fufu!"* *"Hai!* (yes, sir)" *"Patapata!"* *"Hai!"* They are sent to bed tired and hungry while the master prepares to toast *mochi*. But it's wonderful to watch the light dawning in listeners' faces when Fujita-san acts the master blowing: *"Fu, fu!"* *"Hai!"* The master reluctantly gives that *mochi* to the first apprentice and brushes the ashes off another: *"Pata, pata"* — *"Hai!"*

## Closings

When introduced and performed in this manner, most stories can stand on their own. For some tales and some audiences, however, the introducer may sense the need to confirm briefly that they had grasped the story. "Did you see what happened?" "And so from then on, he had to share the *mochi*." Just take care not to dampen their delight in having understood without a translator.

## WHAT DOESN'T WORK

### Stories That Don't Work

Both Fujita-san and I have found that we must sacrifice about 80 percent of our favorite stories in order to work with foreign audiences. Long, complex plots must be left at home. Stories that hinge on a sudden pun or punch line lose their punch if it has to be translated. Tales thick with unfamiliar symbolism and exotic traditional behaviors usually require too much explanation for a live performance. Much as we love them, they don't travel well. Fujita-san and I pride ourselves on our word-spinning skills, but virtuoso verbal performance is lost on people who don't understand the words. Clever dialogue? Forget it. Eloquent descriptions? No way. The 20 percent of stories that survive our ruthless winnowing process have become leaner and shorter as we cut unessential verbiage. If they still fall flat, we drop them.

### Style That Doesn't Work

Some traditional ethnic storytelling styles and some tellers are undemonstrative in the extreme. They sit motionless, seldom even raising a hand for emphasis. (I wonder if this style evolved in a tradition of nighttime telling?) There's no "dance" to see, and unless the teller's voice is dynamic and expressive, there's no "melody" either — just the words. I have read about avid folklore fans who deeply appreciated the authentic recitations of such a teller, but I fear that our general audiences can get very little out of it. If

you are working with a stoic foreign teller, you may need a skilled interpreter to provide a detailed translation for your listeners. But I fear people
may attend only to the English and become restless during the foreign
teller's portion.

I saw for myself the difference style can make at a "Tellabration!" in
Japan. The program featured Fujita-san and seven revivalist Japanese tellers
who wore lovely traditional costumes but had been trained in a style we
suspect was derived from American library schools of the 1950s: words only,
no vocal tricks, no gestures. Although they had lovely voices and very clear
pronunciation, I understood almost nothing of their tales. Funny? Tragic?
Clever? No clues. In contrast, when Fujita-san told a story I had never
heard her perform in the States, I followed it effortlessly.

Afterward, at supper with her daughter Junco, whose English is very fluent, I begged Fujita-san to retell those stories in Japanese to Junco so that
she could translate what I had missed. As Fujita-san revived each story into
her own lively folk style, adding gestures and facial expression as well as
vocal turns, I didn't need Junco's translation!

## CONCLUSION

Storytelling is more than words. If the story (or the teller's style) depends
totally on the words, see other chapters for advice on working with translators. But if you carefully select short, straightforward plots and the teller
adds vocal melody and facial/gestural dance to the verbal lyrics, you can
trust audiences of all ages to follow a performance introduced with a short
synopsis in their own language. They may not understand the words, but
they'll understand the story!

---

## TWO RIVAL SNAKES—*HEBI NO KUIAI*
### by Hiroko Fujita and Fran Stallings

*This story would be told entirely in Japanese in their performances.
But this is an English translation, with some of the Japanese sound
effects included.*

Here is a story from Hiroko-san's repertoire. When this is told in Japanese
Hiroko-san creates the meanings almost entirely with her body language, as
described by Fran below.

Once upon a time in a certain place, there were two mountains and on the first mountain there lived a baby snake.

First he was small, so he ate some bugs, and he grew bigger and bigger

—big enough to eat a frog and a mouse.

He grew bigger and bigger

—big enough to eat a rabbit and a weasel.

He grew bigger and bigger

—big enough to eat a fox and a monkey.

He grew bigger and bigger and bigger

—big enough to eat a deer and a wild boar.

He curled his huge body around the first mountain and took a nap.
On the second mountain there lived another baby snake.
First he was small, so he ate some bugs, and he grew bigger and bigger

—big enough to eat a frog and a mouse.

He grew bigger and bigger

—big enough to eat a rabbit and a weasel.

He grew bigger and bigger

—big enough to eat a fox and a monkey.

He grew bigger and bigger and bigger

—big enough to eat a deer and a wild boar

until there was nothing left on his mountain but clouds, which are no good to eat.

So that snake raised his head and looked for a nice place to get some more food. He thought he saw a lot of deer and wild boars on the first mountain. "Good, I will move there."

So that snake came down from his mountain,

*zuru zuru, nyoro nyoro* (sound of a snake slithering)

to the first mountain

*zuru zuru, nyoro nyoro.*

But on this mountain there was already a big snake.
The first snake woke up, saw the other snake, and said, "What did you come here for?"
The second snake said, "I came to live here, so you get out please."
"What are you talking about? I have lived here all my life. I'll never leave. Go back where you came from!"
"No, I came here from far away. I can't go back. You get out."
"No, I won't move. You go back!"
"No, you get out of here."
The second snake stopped arguing and bit the tail of the first snake.
But the first snake wouldn't give up, so it bit the tail of the second snake.
The two big snakes made a big circle, head to tail, head to tail.
The second snake bit the first one,

*amu amu, amu amu* (munching sound)

and then the first snake bit the second,

*amu amu, amu amu* again and again,
*amu amu, amu amu*
and *amu amu, amu amu* . . .

They wouldn't stop fighting. They wouldn't stop biting.
I don't know how long it took them, but

*amu amu amu* and *amu amu amu*

only their two heads were left.
The second snake said, "I can't give up," and opened his mouth as large as he could with his last strength. But the first snake said, "I can't give up, either," and opened his mouth as large as he could with his last strength.
And so they ate each other up.
There was nothing left at all.
*Oshimai* (That's that).

## Fujita-san's Comments

"I plan to eat you but we are both destroyed."

There are many examples like this in the world, don't you think?

When I told this story at a college, a student made a wonderful picture scroll for me. Such big snakes didn't fit in a picture book so she used a scroll to show it. The picture of the snake was wonderful, and the changing scenes, showing the two snakes biting each other, were also wonderful. I was so glad that she made my poor oral story into wonderful pictures like this. But the snake that I draw in my head is so huge that I can't draw it in the limits of paper. This story ends with both of them gone, and I thought that makes an interesting picture, but it is more interesting when you see it in your head.

## Fran's Comments

We often use this short story to begin programs for adults and older students who might be offended by "baby" visual aids like puppets and pictures. My English synopsis ends when only the heads remain, "and you will see what happened." And they do, thanks to Fujita-san's eloquent hand gestures. After this success, they relax and enjoy the rest of the program—even when we bring out puppets and pictures!

Fujita-san uses her two hands to represent the snakes. When the snakes are tiny, only the tips of her fingers open to eat bugs and mice. When they are big, the whole hands open. Her arms represent the snakes' bodies: the right "head" biting the left "tail" at the shoulder; the left "head" biting the right "tail" at the elbow. When at last only the two "heads" (hands) are left, they open wide wide and come together—clap!—leaving nothing but empty palms. *Oshimai.*

*Chapter 5*

# One Teller, One Story, Two Languages

Many skilled bilingual tellers perform in two languages at once. They have developed various techniques for flipping back and forth between the languages. Here four Spanish-English speakers discuss the techniques they have found useful. I was fortunate to hear Joe Hayes telling bilingually at the King County Library System StoryFest International in Bellevue, Washington one year. Joe speaks very slowly. And even though he is telling the entire story *twice*, his tellings are totally mesmerizing. Both English and Spanish speakers were entranced throughout the entire performance. And, of course, his slow pace allowed those of us with fledgling Spanish skills to at least *think* we were understanding his Spanish.

During a performance at the South Mountain Community College in Phoenix, I was swept away by the total joy of Ricardo Provencio's bilingual telling of that old tale in which a cat teaches her children the value of a second language. Ricardo had us all barking up a storm as the *gato* scared off the *perro* again and again . . . in two languages.

Olga Loya is well known on the storytelling festival circuit for her delightful tales, but not everyone has had the chance to hear her do her amazing bilingual telling, in which she flips fluently from one language to another. And Venezuelan-born Angela Lloyd tells of her changing sense of story, as she switches back and forth between languages. Each of these Spanish/English-speaking tellers has developed a unique method of communicating across the language barrier.

Michael Harvey tells in both English and Welsh. He shares here his techniques for interlacing the Welsh language into stories . . . sometimes for English-speaking audiences . . . sometimes for Welsh speakers (who also speak English). The beauty of the language inspires him to do this difficult work. And Martin Ellrodt talks of a first attempt at bilingual German/English telling while on tour in Hong Kong.

## TWO TALES AT ONCE
by Joe Hayes

*New Mexican teller Joe Hayes tells fluently in both English and Spanish, often sharing the entire tale in both languages at once. In his bilingual tellings, Joe moves from one language to the other, easing in and out, often within the same sentence. At no point is any listener left behind. In fact the tellings are so flawless that listeners believe they have understood both languages. Here Joe reveals some of his secrets and offers suggestions for other tellers.*

**Could you comment for me about the sorts of choices you have to make to do this?**

The first thing I should say is that bilingual telling combining English and Spanish in the United States is probably different from combining any other language with English. Almost all U.S. Americans have had some exposure to Spanish. Just about every child can count to five or ten in Spanish. I think this makes bilingual Spanish/English telling easier than any other bilingual telling.

The audience dictates an extremely important choice you have to make. There are English-speaking audiences with a fair knowledge of Spanish, and others with very little. Certain English-speaking audiences have little knowledge but a lot of interest in Spanish. Other audiences show very little or no interest. Some audiences are made up of monolingual English speakers and monolingual Spanish speakers. Others consist of bilingual English/Spanish speakers. Most frequently I work with audiences combining monolingual English speakers and bilingual Spanish/English speakers with varying command of each language.

The hardest audience is one with some monolingual English and some monolingual Spanish speakers. You pretty much have to do the entire story in both languages. This is the most challenging form of bilingual telling. It requires command of the whole story in both languages. And it requires a real sense of how to vary the length of sections told in the one language before switching to the other. It can work, and I do it, but it's a challenge. One trick is to tell a certain part of the story in the one language and then, in addition to translating that section, go a bit beyond it in the second language. It sort of switches the lead and keeps both language speakers happy.

**Do some kinds of stories seem to work better bilingually?**

For the most part, formula stories, stories with very repetitive structure, lend themselves best to bilingual storytelling. If you learn all the repeated elements in both languages, once you establish them, it doesn't matter which language you tell them in. The listeners know what you are saying.

**Do you find it hard to hold audiences while performing in two languages?**

I find listeners to be delighted by the use of two languages. But if you try to plod along, telling a block in English, a block in Spanish, a block in English, a block in Spanish, you'll have trouble holding the audience. One of the secrets of bilingual telling . . . actually of all storytelling, although it's not much emphasized . . . is rhythm. You can often make a statement given twice feel like one rhythmic whole. This is something people in linguistic interface areas such as the Southwest do all the time. They'll say, "*¿Qué pasó¿*, Johnny, what happened?" as one statement. The rhythm of a telling is such an important part of holding the audience's attention—both the rhythm of the speech and the rhythm of the story elements as it unfolds.

**When did you start doing this and how did you teach yourself to tell in this format?**

I mixed Spanish and English in stories from the time I first started telling, from before I ever imagined I would be a "storyteller." As you know, learning to tell stories isn't a matter of teaching yourself or of having someone teach you; it's a matter of discovering how you can tell stories. If anyone taught me it was the kids I told stories to. Observing their reactions and noticing what was making the story work for them, my style of telling the stories evolved. Another storytelling secret: To become a real storyteller, you have to be totally sensitive to the listeners. I also drew a lot from my life experience in a dual-language context. I knew the natural way in which people mix languages.

**Do you prefer to tell in only one language?**

No, not at all. The use of two languages enriches the story for me too. The only time I don't use any Spanish in any of my stories is when I tell to Native American kids for whom English is already a second language. Once I did tell stories to Russian kids who were just learning English, but I snuck in a little Spanish and they enjoyed it.

But I don't use Spanish in all my stories. Primarily, I use it in stories derived from Hispanic culture. That just seems natural. Of course when I tell in Latin America, I have to use Spanish for all the stories. In that case, I often look for places to slip in English, which the listeners really appreciate.

Here are Joe's suggestions to help create a bilingual telling:

## Adaptations for Bilingual Telling

1. Find a good reference person who can help you translate words and phrases.

2. Choose a tale. Look for a lot of repetition and predictable language and structure.

   A. Cumulative tale
   B. Repeated dialogue
   C. Refrain
   D. Repeated series of events

3. Identify places in the story where a second language can be inserted without interrupting the momentum of the tale.

   | | |
   |---|---|
   | names of characters | repeated dialogue |
   | cumulative runs | characters' speech |
   | items in a series | item that is focus of attention |
   | refrain | silly or fun event |

4. After locating all the places where a second language could be used, select the ones you feel most comfortable with and that seem most entertaining or educational. Your comfort level with the second language will also determine what and how much you choose.

5. Work out translations of selected elements. Try to make the second language and the translation fit together into a single rhythmic whole.

6. The second language occurs at fun places in the story. This helps nonspeakers feel more comfortable with and open to the second language. It makes speakers of the second language feel proud.

7. If there are speakers and nonspeakers in the group, try to give the second language first so that speakers have an edge on nonspeakers. Again, this gives them a sense of pride and an awareness that their second language is really an asset. Sometimes let speakers translate for nonspeakers.

8. Use nonverbal language to reinforce meaning. Be consistent with gestures. This helps establish a connection between the word and its meaning, rather than the word and its translation. Nonverbal sounds (knocking, creaking, animal noises) reinforce meaning.

---

## A CHOREOGRAPHED LANGUAGE MIX
### by Ricardo Provencio

*I was fortunate to hear Ricardo Provencio tell his version of the tale of the bilingual cat in Phoenix a few years ago. He kept up a rapid-fire stream of both English and Spanish and had his audience . . . many of whom understood both languages . . . barking and laughing with delight. Here he shares his techniques for preparing a story for bilingual use.*

Most printed stories are in either English or Spanish, though there are some exceptions, with more bilingual books starting to appear on the market. At any rate, when I pick a story to tell, I usually follow this model:

- First I learn the story by embedding the story line and characters in my memory. If it's a long or more complicated story, I may write it out in outline form or do a mind-map diagram for myself.
- Then I like to use Spanish at the beginning of most of my stories to pull in, plant, start, transplant the listeners to where the story and I are coming from. Sometimes it's just a opening phrase or two or three. And I try to put lots of energy, passion, excitement, in my voice and physical movements, again to move the listener to a different place and time. On a few occasions when I want to make a stronger statement of place, time, or character, I may use a longer Spanish opening for two to three minutes or more . . . but I usually find most English-dominant audiences get uncomfortable with this and I lose them with too much Spanish. For Spanish-speaking audiences, I will use more Spanish in my storytelling and less English. Makes sense, doesn't it?
- Then I look for strategic places for inserting Spanish. I try hard not to translate word for word . . . English to Spanish throughout the story. I do translate some but try to not overdo it because I find it tiresome both for me as the teller and for the listener.
- I usually use less Spanish toward the end of my stories. I find that most listeners have moved to the bilingual and/or Spanish time, place, and character, and I do not need to use as much Spanish . . . but still need to keep them there with a simple word or phrase to refresh or keep them in the story.
- Depending on the story, I may need to do some setup at the beginning of a story for repetition or translating or explaining a Spanish word or phrase. Or I may insert this later in the story and look for a way to step out of story and ask for audience participation.

---

## TELLING A TALE BILINGUALLY
by Olga Loya

*In this article previously published in* Storytelling Magazine, *Olga Loya shares her techniques for telling bilingually. I was impressed by Olga's skills during performances for children at the Bothell Library some years ago. Olga managed to switch between languages fluently in a seamless stream of story sense, which carried all of the children along.*

I would like to share with you my technique for telling stories bilingually and my reasons for doing it that way. While I tell in Spanish and English and will refer to these two languages throughout the article, these same principles could be used for any other combination of languages.

When you first start to tell bilingual stories, it is a good idea to find a simple tale so that you can concentrate on deciding which words you will say in which language, rather than concentrating on trying to remember a complicated plot. Like with any other storytelling, your first (and sometimes hardest) task is to find a suitable story.

When you find a story you like, read it out loud. See if you can hear the rhythm of the story. Then start thinking about how much of the tale you will put in each language. When I am practicing a story, I first go through it entirely in English if it is written in that language or entirely in Spanish if it is written in that language. I read it silently and then out loud. I try starting the story in the language it is *not* written in. Usually if the story is written in Spanish, I translate in into English and then I add in the Spanish.

Many of my performances are mainly in English with some sentences and phrases in Spanish. If I have an audience that has some listeners who speak Spanish and some who only speak English, I will do the whole story in both languages. This is the most difficult performance of all because the teller has to think in two languages while keeping the focus of the story and not interrupting the flow of the narrative.

If the audience is Spanish speaking, then I tell the stories entirely in Spanish. This is my favorite mode of telling because I can just abandon myself to the beautiful sound of the Spanish words.

When I perform bilingually, I always tell first in Spanish and then in English. It is an interesting and wonderful phenomenon to have the Spanish-speaking listeners laugh first and then repeat the joke in English and have everyone laugh. It is very powerful for the Spanish-speaking audience to have a chance to understand something first here in English-dominated America where so often they feel left out.

There are many different techniques of doing bilingual storytelling. Some performers do long segments in one language and then do the translation into the other language. Some tell the whole story in Spanish and then repeat it in English, or vice versa. What I prefer to do is simultaneous translations.

I do this because personally I don't have a long attention span, and I don't like listening for a prolonged period of time without knowing what is happening. I believe many listeners would be as bored as I would be by this style, so instead of relying only on the words, I sometimes rely on the physicality of the story. I try to find a way of moving or a stance to help people understand a phrase. For example, in one story there are three animals having a dialogue with a female cockroach. When I am speaking as the animals, I always stand in a certain way. When I am speaking as the cockroach, I stand in a different way. Since the dialogue is the same between the cockroach and each of the animals, the last time I do not have to translate it into English because my body shows who is talking and what they are saying. Also I look for a certain tone of voice for a word or phrase and keep that tone consistently.

When I have found a tale to work with, I go over the whole story and begin to play with it. I try phrases and individual words in English and in Spanish and keep playing until I have found the right balance of languages. I remain flexible so that if there is largely an English-speaking audience, I don't add too much Spanish. This balance changes for a largely Spanish-speaking audience. Take a few lines such as: *Había una vez una Cucarachita que pensaba que era muy fea. Once there was a little cockroach who thought she was very ugly. Se miraba en el espejo y decía, "Ay, soy tan fea."* She would look in the mirror and say, "Oh, I am so ugly." One way to say these lines is as they are written above.

Another way would be to translate only some of the words into Spanish: Once there was a little *Cucarachita*, cockroach, who thought she was *fea*, ugly. She would look in the mirror and say, "*Ay, soy tan fea*. Oh, I am so ugly."

What I try to do is keep the rhythm going from the English to the Spanish and back again so that it sounds like one story rather than two separate ones. It's important to not speak so fast that the Spanish and English run together.

I also play with not only the translation but also the style it is written in. If it is mainly in the third person, I change much of it into dialogue. Often I add participation. For example, for a myth titled "*La Diosa Hambrienta*, The Hungry Goddess," I use the statement, "*Tengo Hambre*. I am hungry." I tell the audience that I want them to hear the sentence in a *llanto*, wail. We practice wailing the words. When I tell the story, I use my drum to let the audience know when it is time to wail.

Whenever I am using participation in another language in a story, I begin by telling the listeners the words I will want them to say. I then translate the words so they will understand what they are saying. I then have them say each word separately and then together as a sentence or phrase. Then I say the words in the rhythm I would like them to use and have the audience repeat the words using my rhythm. I like to have the listeners say the words often enough in the story so that they are comfortable with them and will possibly remember them later.

A new area of bilingual translation I have been playing with is saying something in Spanish and having the translation in the response. An example from one of my stories would be:

Snake Woman said, "*¿Quien eres y qué quieres?*"
Luna answered, "My name is Luna, and I am looking for a magician."

The English-speaking listeners then understand that Snake Woman was asking who Luna was and what she wanted. In this type of bilingual translation, it is important to have two distinct characters speaking so that the audience is clear about who is talking. Otherwise it can get confusing.

As you can see, there are many things to think about when telling bilingually. It comes down to finding a story you love, feeling comfortable with the two languages you are using, and playing with the story until you find the right rhythm for yourself. Then you can tell the story, and let the audience enjoy it.[*]

---

### SOMOS EL BARCO—WE ARE THE BOAT
by Angela Lloyd

*Angela Lloyd talks of her innate relationship to her native Spanish language and reminds us of the importance of silence in communication.*

I was raised in Caracas, Venezuela, from birth to fourteen years, 1954 to 1968. My parents are American, my mother, a composer-pianist, and my father an engineer who loved to sing. I grew up with three languages, intertwined: English, Spanish, and Musica. My first songs were in Spanish. I have recently become aware, living here in California, that when I am with someone who also has Spanish as a first language I can feel it in my body, an inherent recognition, and without a thought I move into Spanish. As a storyteller and musician, I have moved organically between the two languages, just as I do in my ordinary day.

If there are Spanish native speakers in the room I am telling in, I will move between the two languages inside the story. I will spontaneously often make one or more of the characters a Spanish speaker (not always the same character). All of his or her dialogue will be in Spanish; and all the other characters become bilingual and can understand each other, the sister, the king, or the elder stranger who asks for bread or offers help.

In 1979, I was a member of an Equity Repertory Company with the Players State Theatre in Coconut Grove, Florida. We staged three original bilingual plays for school-age audiences that winter and spring, and this was the gift:

A character would ask a question in one language, Spanish, and another character would answer in English, and everyone on the room would know what had just happened.

Reprinted from *Storytelling Magazine*, May–June 1999, with permission of the National Storytelling Network.

For example:

*"¿Quieres ir al baile conmigo esta noche?"*
I would love to go to the dance with you!
*Te puedo cojer a las siete.*
Great! I'll see you at seven!

I feel fortunate for that early exposure. The writers taught us that we could, by design in the writing, have a multilingual society on stage—no need to labor as translators.

Personally, I have always had difficulty listening to bilingual tellers who moved from one language to another. I recognized a few years ago it had to do with making that shift within the same breath.

Each language has its own rhythm, meter, tempo, and phrasing; and being a musician, my experience was similar to listening to a singer changing rhythm and meter mid-phrase. So there was very little space, it sounded interrupted, rushed . . . and I could not relax as long as the "musical measure" was incomplete.

As a performer, I make a point to remember that there is time and space and silence that we can rest in; this always benefits the listeners. They are new travelers to the story, it is a new place, and they will appreciate the chance to take a look around, to settle in to where we are in the story without being rushed into the next moment of the story.

Many, many times I have told a story in English and Spanish that I had not prepared to tell bilingually, and often I've come upon an image I need the Spanish for. So I freely ask someone in the audience to give the phrase or words. This is always fun, because it is participatory, is generally appreciated, and builds community in the company of strangers.

Other times, if the story is complicated, as the audience arrives, I'll ask a teacher who speaks Spanish if I can look to her specifically during the story for vocabulary. This offers her a heads up and lets her know I am comfortable asking for help from the stage.

As a musician, listener, poet, composer, live performance–teller/celebrant . . . I am committed to:

Creating a relaxed situation for listeners through language.
Poetry in Spanish—delicious, and memorized.
Story crossing the bridge to song: this trusty vehicle, the art and Arc—
having sailed many seas, endured many shores—will carry us back to
ourselves.

As for the Listening, the sea of silence has waves of energy.
Open hearts beating the ancient diversity of pulses and rhythms.

An honored activity, this telling and listening—rooted in silence, rooted
   in Home.
Home: resting in our bodies, "breathing together," as Ed Stivender says.
"Open rest" I call it—however restless the room often feels.

All of this is to say

that we are ultimately participating in the gift of being together
and being in a community of languages via song, story, poetry, musica—
and what better way to go Home
than through our mother—the language/s we were raised with,
and tongue,
the mother tongue!

---

## WHEN SOME SPEAK WELSH AND ALL SPEAK ENGLISH
### by Michael Harvey

*Michael Harvey, a Welsh teller working in Great Britain and beyond,
has found various ways to communicate in two languages at once.
Note his comments on using recaps, changing styles for different
languages, and telling in Welsh without translation just for the
beauty of it.*

I work in English and Welsh. One of the dynamics of working in a
minority language like Welsh is that almost all the native speakers are bilingual, whereas the majority language is spoken by everyone. This means that
there is a tendency for mixed groups to turn to English because "everyone
understands English." This does seem like an impasse sometimes, because
the tensions surrounding language and identity can throw up issues of exclusion or imperialism, and everyone ends up in a bad mood.

One of the things I like to do for mixed bilingual/monoglot audiences is
bilingual telling. This can include straight tellings in either language with
English introduction for the Welsh stories for the monoglot speakers, or
telling a story in Welsh in bits, with English preview for each chunk. I
try to make the register of the telling different . . . often much lighter and
throwaway in style in the English bits . . . but cue the non-Welsh speakers
with gestures so that they know "Ah, we're in that bit now." Because they
remember the gesture from the English telling. Changing styles with different languages helps with variety, and also because of the different flavor of
the telling, I don't end up tripping myself up by thinking, "Hang on . . .
haven't I said this before!" Well, not so often anyway.

One thing I love to do is tell a story purely in Welsh and get the audience to translate in small groups. The audience members like this because they get a bit of vicarious touchy-feely (snuggling up close and whispering in each other's ears) and everyone is respected and included. Strangely, the more efficient and professional the translation is, the more it seems to cut across the event.

At a Welsh language session in Beyond the Border every year, we tell with translation from other tellers. We don't rehearse, because the translation is part of the performance. It can be very moving, and the listeners love being part of it and even join in on repetitive bits as they get the hang of it. They also enjoy the little arguments that occur when it goes a bit awry.

I very rarely "translate" my storytelling but rather address my telling to different audiences within the group in front of me. My most common experience, as a speaker of a minority language, is of working with an audience 100 percent of whom understand one of the languages I am using and a smaller group that understands both. I usually contextualize the telling in English and use Welsh for passages within that context and rely on the monoglot audience's context-guessing powers to fill in the gaps. In Wales many people also have a passive understanding of Welsh, and this gives them the pleasure of being able to follow a narrative in their second language. I attempt not to repeat myself so that all the people are listening all the time. I try and weave recaps into the narrative so the audience is not too aware of it happening. This means that I am dealing with one audience rather than two, which is very important for me as a teller. I also use Welsh for audiences that I know will have no Welsh for material that is "very Welsh." When I do Taliesin I really do feel that the words coming out of his mouth have to be in Welsh; and I perform *Culhwch and Olwen* with a musician and singer where we use the language musically. All the songs are in Welsh and we do some of the formalized descriptive passages in a bilingual format.

---

## GERMAN/ENGLISH TELLING IN HONG KONG
### by Martin Ellrodt

*I ran into Martin Ellrodt in Hong Kong where he was a guest of the German-Swiss International School. Though Martin usually tells in only one language at a time, this situation required him to flip into a bilingual telling. I asked him about the experience.*

## Consecutive Interpretation

Actually I haven't done a lot of bilingual telling or telling in German to non-German audiences either. In the Hong Kong school I told in German to children with German as a foreign language, but needed to tell in English *and* German to the mixed audiences. In the case of the latter, I felt somewhat at ease, because I'd done work as an interpreter many years ago. So what I used was the technique of consecutive interpretation; that is, telling story bits between half a minute and a whole, first in one language and then in the other, but the bits were not congruent in respect of their content. I would advance further in the story in English than I had in German, then resume the German telling, but again advance further than before in English, and so on. It worked well, and I had the impression that the audience, whose language was not spoken at that time, noticed that more was told than they already knew, and could start to guess about the plot and confirm or discard their guesses later. Yet, by alternating the advance, it was not only one group that always had to wait for the translation.

*Chapter 6*

# On the Translator's Role

Those who translate for us have difficult tasks. Especially when they take it seriously and strive for the perfect translation. Livia de Almeida tells of her terror at taking on the role of translator and her joy at seeing the tale through the eyes of another teller. "Seeing the backside of the tapestry," as she explains it.

Dr. Wajuppa Tossa writes of her trials and tribulations . . . and her joys . . . trying to translate this teller into Lao or Thai. I do speak at a rapid clip. I try to speak more slowly when working with a translator, but when I become accustomed to someone like Wajuppa, I sometimes forget and speed up to U.S.-style telling. She is such a quick translator that she has seldom stumbled, even then.

Masako Sueyoshi speaks of translating myself and other American tellers into Japanese. Masako works hard at her translation from story texts sent ahead of time. She wants plenty of time to rehearse them before performances . . . and turns out an amazingly fleet-footed presentation once onstage.

Paula Martín, of Buenos Aires, has had experience doing bilingual telling, translating for English-speaking tellers, and translating for publication . . . both English to Spanish and Spanish to English. She speaks of all these tasks and of the aesthetic differences between English and Spanish.

I had the chance to experience the translator's role once myself. Elvia Pérez came from Cuba to Vancouver, British Columbia, to perform. It took her host, Dunc Shields, a couple of days to arrange a bilingual translator for her, so I got the opportunity to translate her evening performance for the Vancouver Storytelling Guild. What a joy it was! Though my Spanish is not the best, I knew the stories she was telling and had heard her tell them before. So it was easy to accompany her lively tellings with equally lively English. I did enjoy this. It felt like singing along with someone. And was even more fun that telling myself . . . because she had the task of remembering and shaping the story!

# THE BACKSIDE OF THE TAPESTRY
by Livia de Almeida

*Livia de Almeida has had experience translating English tellers into her native Portuguese* and *of translating a Portuguese-speaking teller into English. She compares her tandem-translating work to jazz . . . and to rhythmically tossing a ball back and forth.*

One of the first notions I was told about storytelling was that it was virtually untranslatable. A truly good performer, I heard, would be able to overcome any language barriers by the sheer force of the art. These considerations brought great unquiet to my mind, as I attended the National Storytelling Festival in Jonesborough, Tennessee, in 1997. There was so much we could learn from the English-speaking performers, and there should be a way to be able to share this experience with the largest audience possible. I felt that without translation, this pleasure would be limited to the few who were already interested enough in storytelling, whereas I wanted to be able to show the art to a new audience. During the festival, I saw tandem telling for the first time in my life and it dawned on me that this might be a way to bring bilingual storytelling to life. Still I could not see a practical way to make this work out.

Only one year later, when Dr. Margaret Read MacDonald came to perform in Rio de Janeiro, I had the chance to experience tandem telling. As we went through her stories, I learned that I had to be as much of a performer as she, blending my own style to hers, playing in harmony. I wasn't supposed to translate the story line first, but to do a tandem performance, translating sentence by sentence. Quite unconsciously, I started mirroring her gestures and movements. I also realized that, more than a perfect word-by-word translation, what we both needed to make this succeed was rhythm; English and Portuguese had to flow in the cadence needed by the story, like a nonstop ball game. During the Tellabration event in Rio and São Paulo—I have lost count of how many performances we did, for small and large audiences—on one occasion, in the Republic Museum, we had over 1,000 people, according to museum estimates. And it certainly worked. I definitely acquired a taste for the translating job.

For a novice storyteller like myself, it was as if I had been allowed to view the backside of an embroidery: the stitches, the knots. I was generously invited to take a peek into the world of someone else's imagination. In many ways, this experience helped me acquire a sense of awareness of my time on stage. Performing with Margie was just like playing jazz; I had to be very attentive to get what was coming next and improvise. But above all,

I had an enormous amount of fun with the story and the audiences. The next year, I had the chance to translate Heather Forrest, also during Tellabration. The fun was the same. I even translated some of the lyrics of her songs into Portuguese and sang along, though my musical abilities leave much to be desired.

So far, it had been quite comfortable for me. I had been translating English into Portuguese, my mother language. Then I was called in to do the opposite: translate into English the words of Roberto Carlos Ramos. He is one of the most amazing storytellers I have ever seen in action, with a very physical, very unique style; the king of free improvisation and a specialist in jump tales. How on earth would I be able to follow him and not bore audiences to death by being redundant? And more, would I be able to find the right words to convey his rich imagery?

I have to confess on our first round of performances in the Seattle area, back in 1999, I was really insecure. I discovered really fast that the fun was all there. On our very first set of shows, I realized in a very practical way that I didn't have to echo his "jump" moments. I jumped myself. The frights never came the same way or at the same moment, and it worked on stage to show that I was genuinely jumping, like the audience. Of course, I stuttered and sometimes was really on the verge of not finding the right word. Again, I realized that rhythm should dictate my work, and that the voice, tone, and way of pronouncing each sentence would be very, very important. The audiences would certainly be listening to me, but with Roberto's colorful style, they would have their eyes glued on him!

With Roberto, no story was ever the same. But as we played along, we started interacting more and more. Sometimes I would even playfully scold him for a fright. Sometimes, he would slip a phrase in English and make fun of me. With Roberto, I felt I was much of my own persona on stage. There was no possible way to emulate his style. I never even tried. Roberto allowed me to become a kind of accomplice on stage, someone in the know. Sometimes during performance, we exchanged glances as if we were telling each other: "Oh, boy, they don't have any idea of what is coming next and it is going to be so much fun!" Sometimes my role was to be more of a commentator of the action, since his own physical style of performing made words secondary on occasion. By looking on the backside of Roberto's embroidery, I learned about timing in a very practical way.

I have thoroughly enjoyed my experiences in translating storytelling. For a while, it was as though I was being allowed into my partner's imagination. It was a trip to uncharted territory. And I felt I was inside the story and always in wonderful company.

## PROBLEMS AND PLEASURES OF STORY TRANSLATION
by Wajuppa Tossa

*Dr. Wajuppa Tossa of Mahasarakham University in northeastern
Thailand tells of her work translating in an educational setting. She
wished to teach her students to share stories in Lao, the original
language of Isaan, which is now being replaced by Bangkok Thai.
Her intent was to engender pride in their own culture and language.*

### A Storytelling Project to Revitalize Language

In 1995, I initiated a project entitled, "Storytelling, a Means to Maintain
and Revitalize Local Literature in Northeast Thailand." I received support
from the Fulbright Foundation, which sent me Dr. Margaret Read Mac-
Donald, a storyteller, folklorist, and children's literature specialist. In this
project, I was trying to engender pride in cultural heritage among children
in northeast Thailand by using northeast Thai folktales and storytelling.
These tales would be told in Lao or in other local dialects. We recruited
twenty university students and trained them to collect folktales, adapt them
for performances, and tell them in story-theater style. Dr. MacDonald could
understand and speak some Thai, but not enough to tell stories in Thai or
Lao. A few students could understand English well; they might be able to
understand almost everything in English, but a lot of students were not
English majors and some were first-year students. Thus, their English was
not sufficient for them to understand the entire lecture in English. So, I
became an official translator for her lectures and storytelling performances.

### Teaching Bilingually

For the project we met with the students late in the day, after their regular
classes. Dr. MacDonald would teach them about folklore and storytelling,
such as definitions of folktales, folktale motifs, how to collect folktales, and
how to adapt them for storytelling performances. I had the honor of translating all of these lectures. Dr. M. wanted to make sure that students understood everything, so the translation was done line by line. She spoke one
sentence in English and I did it in Lao. It went very well. Students understood the lessons well. When she told stories as examples to illustrate her
points and to give the students models of storytelling, I did the translation
the same way, line by line.

### The Joys of Speaking Lao

It was so much fun for the students to hear Lao translation, because it is not spoken nor has been allowed to be spoken in public. Lao, a very down-to-earth and emphatic language with a lot of descriptive and visual sounds, is my first language; it is the language of my soul. I translated with all my heart. It was enjoyable for me to recall all the subtleties of the language to use in the translation to make it interesting to the tired students. They became more confident and assertive in using the language to retell the stories or to communicate with me during the project activities. I experienced much pleasure in the translating, as both the contents and the stories were new to me.

### Translation Techniques Used

In the sessions with the students, the translation went on informally. Thus, I could stop Dr. M. when I did not understand something, she would explain it, and then I would continue with the translation. After gaining familiarity with the ways of Dr. M.'s storytelling, I began to feel more comfortable translating. When Dr. M., on the other hand, became familiar with my ways of translation, she began to treat me as a character in the story. We became tandem storytellers, adding voices, actions, and emotions as the story allowed.

### Giving the Students Practice

During the time that we trained students, we also provided them with opportunities to tell stories in authentic environments. By taking them to schools nearby to tell stories, the students got chances to practice telling stories in front of an auditorium full of children and teachers. Dr. M. also told stories, as she wanted to show our students how to manage the audience, and again I was the official translator. Having a famous storyteller in a village school was a great hit, and so the children and teachers asked Dr. M. to tell even more stories. The stories that she chose were simple and easy for young Thai children. The translation went well in these sessions.

### Misunderstandings Do Happen

By the end of the first part of Dr. M's stay at the university, we thought of a plan of giving workshops on the preservation and dissemination of folktales and storytelling to teachers and the general public. In all sessions, Dr.

M. would both lecture and tell stories to inform the participants about how to use storytelling to accomplish these purposes. All our workshops began with an opening story. Dr. M. would choose from a variety of new stories for the opening story, and I thought I could manage. However, one time she told the story "Lifting the Sky." I could understand the story well until the point when the Creator left the sky too low and people could not go around easily. They kept bumping their heads on the sky. Some people even went to play in the sky when it was not the proper time. At this spot in the story, I heard Dr. M. say, "And all the sheep came for a meeting to solve the problem." So I translated. As the story continued, I began to feel that the sheep could not do all the thinking and planning. Then, I also heard the word *elders*; they could not be sheep. So, I stopped Dr. M. and asked whether they were *sheep* or *chiefs*. And, of course, they were not sheep. So, I promptly corrected myself and the participants thought it was great fun. They were all very supportive and understanding of the mistake I had made, but I certainly did not want to make the same kind of mistake again. And I didn't.

### Playing with the Translations

Later, when I got to a point of the story I did not understand, I made sure to ask Dr. M. to clarify it, doing it in a fun way so it would not ruin the mood of the story. Sometimes, I would add some Lao onomatopoeia instead of the American word. For example, when the dog went, "woof, woof," I would say the dog went, "hong, hong." It was always fun translating Dr. M. as she is a very animated storyteller and I tackled the challenge to be as animated in the Lao translation. In one of the workshops we organized, an Australian participant asked me to translate her story during the story-swap session. She told the story of a hero fighting with the sun, the moon, the wind, and the cloud. She made no sounds to illustrate her story and was not animated in her storytelling. So, I translated the very long story the same way she told it. Other workshop participants were very polite but seemed a bit bored. Later another Australian participant asked why I hadn't added any sounds or actions in the translation. So, I explained that it was hard because I was trying to understand the story too. One comment on this incident is that it works out well when the translator and the storyteller have worked together and known each other for a while. Also when the storyteller is inexperienced, it is difficult to translate. However, animated storytellers are easier to translate. The stories with a lot of audience participation provide for tandem storytelling in two languages. This happened when I translated for George Shannon, Jim Wolf, Bruce Hale, and Brian Sturm.*

*\*Editor's note*: All of these tellers visited Dr. Wajuppa Tossa at Mahasarakham University and offered workshops for her students there.

## When the Stories Are Already Known to the Translator

The work mentioned above was the translation of new stories, stories I had not heard before. When it came to stories that I already knew, my translation was even more fun. I tried hard to translate what Dr. M. told, but sometimes I was so caught up in the story's mood that I could not stop where she stopped and went over a little. When she actually said the sentences, I would say to the audience, "I already translated that." The audience thought that was funny. However, I have to be careful not to do that too often. It worked when it was an accident, not an intentional act.

The creativity of the storyteller is another way to make translation entertaining. Dr. M. sometimes would add Thai words that she knew in the story, which I would automatically translate into English. The audience liked it, appreciating that a famous storyteller could speak their language and anticipating what I would do in reaction to that. They enjoyed it when I immediately said the Thai words in English—instead of simply waiting for the next sentence in English to translate. This playful act works only when the storyteller and the translator have known each other for a long time, as both have to be quite quick and witty.

## Keeping Up with a Speeding Teller

Because of Dr. M.'s speed in telling stories, sometimes it would take time for me to translate at my pace. Other times, I would pause to think of what to say and she would assume I had finished. So she would go on. At first I would be panicky and ask her to stop because I had not finished. So she would. Again the audience thought it was funny. In some cases, I would not stop her because that would have ruined the mood of the story. So, I had to think of ways to add important parts of the story that I had not translated. Later, I solved the problem by translating the important part that I had missed before going on to translate new sentences that were not too long or too fast. This worked out well.

## Translating into Thai

In most cases, I would translate English into Lao and it worked out well. However, once we went to tell stories in an area of Surin where students understood only Khmer and Thai. I had one student who could tell stories in Khmer, as it was her dialect in her area. However, when I was available, Dr. M. would rather choose me as her translator. So, I had to translate her stories into central Thai. If I could do the translation to Thai rather than Lao, of course, the children would understand the stories well. However, I did not feel confident because a lot of the playful sounds and words in Lao were lost in Thai. That was only one of the many times I had to translate stories into central Thai instead of Lao, such as when we went to the north, to the south, and to Bangkok for storytelling. I had to practice many times before I could get the translation right. But at least I would translate one story into *Lao* for the audience so that they could hear stories in different ways. Most of the audience liked it, but they could listen to only a story or two in Lao.* Dr. M. would even ask me to do tandem storytelling with her in Singapore and the United States to show the audience that storytelling in two languages would work even when the audience could understand only one of the two languages.

## Using Bilingual Telling to Teach English as a Second Language

After working with Dr. M., I believed that I could use storytelling in two languages in my own storytelling in Thailand. In this way, the Thai listeners could learn English. It worked out very well with the story "Little Cricket Looks for a Husband," an Iranian folktale retold by Nan Gregory from Canada. I also added a Thai/Lao folk song and dance in the story with the subtle translation—the character asking or repeating the sentences in English as a translation. The story is about a little cricket who tries to find a husband that would not beat her when he is angry. When she walks past the different men, they court her by singing (in Lao) the following song:

> *Laa oey chao si pai sai*     [Younger sister, where are you going?]
> *Man pen ta yaan si tai*     [It looks dreadfully dangerous.]
> *Hai nang long sa kon*     [Please stop and sit down here.]

After he sang his love song, without translating, I have the cricket reply:

> "You asked where I am going. I know it is dangerous outside. That's why I am looking for a husband."

And then she would sing:

> *Aay oey nong si pai sai*     [Older brother, where I am going?]
> *Man pen ta yaan si tai*     [I know it is dangerous outside.]
> *Nong si pai ha khuu*     [That's why I am looking for a husband.]

In that way, the audience in Thailand could understand English sentences and the English-speaking audience could understand the English translation done without pausing to translate.

---

*Editor's note: Thai speakers can make out some of what a Lao speaker is saying, but it is difficult.

In using songs and poems from Thai/Lao tradition in storytelling, I feel that I have helped in preserving or revitalizing the language, poetry, and literature. I have also shared some Thai/Lao culture with English-speaking audiences. At the same time, Thai/Lao listeners can learn some English words from the stories.

In translating stories, the translators discover new stories and techniques. The audience also learns to appreciate a new way of telling a story. This can be also useful in language learning. Thus, I use this technique in my teaching of English, and in the preservation of local dialects, such as Lao, hoping they will continue to grow alongside the mainstream central Thai language.

## Cultural Sensitivity as the Translator's Role?

*Here Dr. Wajuppa Tossa discusses altering content for culturally sensitive reasons during translation. One could question whether this is the role of the translator, though translating the "cultures" might properly be considered a translation role.*

When I was vice president for international affairs at Mahasarakham University, I acted as the main interpreter for international scholars who would visit the university. Certain visitors were from a Korean university, and at that time the university did not offer Korean as a major or minor subject. We had to communicate in English. One of the visitors could actually understand and speak some Thai, but not enough for us to do the presentation all in Thai. So, I had the honor of doing the translation for the university president and the administrators in his team. It was an interesting job because I had to listen to the president and staff carefully and screen some information at the same time. Friendly Thai people would ask personal questions, such as How old are you? How much money do you make? Are you married? Would you like to marry a Thai? When these questions came up, I had to think of ways to ask without offending the visitors or embarrassing my own colleagues. By the end of the meeting, the visitor who could understand both Thai and Korean said to me, "You have an interesting way of interpreting." I didn't think much of it, and little did I know that that interesting way of interpreting would come up later in my career as a storyteller.

## TRANSLATING AN ENGLISH SPEAKER INTO JAPANESE
by Masako Sueyoshi

*Masako Sueyoshi has translated many times for Margaret Read MacDonald during their storytelling tours in Japan. She has also translated for American tellers Kate McClelland, Lorna Stengel, and J. G. Pinkerton, among others. She writes here of problems encountered in this work.*

### Problems in Translating Another Teller

There are many difficulties involved in translating an English-speaking teller into Japanese. For example, the word order in English differs from Japanese. In English you say, "I am a girl." In Japanese I say, "I girl am." So, even if I translate your words line by line, I cannot translate word by word.

Sometimes when you tell in English, you use only one word. But I need a whole sentence to make that same sense. Or the opposite might occur. You speak for a whole sentence . . . but the concept in Japanese is conveyed by a single word.

This causes our rhythm . . . our telling tempo . . . to be off. We want to keep the pacing similar . . . but this makes it difficult to do so.

The pacing is important to a good performance. MacDonald tries to make her pacing very clear for the Japanese audiences. We attempt to maintain a strong rhythm in our telling. MacDonald tries not to interrupt my pacing and likewise I to follow hers. This makes a good performance. I try to achieve this every time.

What we do is not just an ordinary translation. We are performing together. This is one story . . . but two storytellers. This is a new form of translation that most other tellers had not tried before we demonstrated it.

Here is one word of caution for this kind of translating, though. The translating teller must keep the pace slow enough for the Japanese listener. MacDonald tends to move more and more rapidly into her stories. If I were to translate as fast as she wants to move, some of the story might be lost on our Japanese listeners. So I have to fight hard not to be swallowed by MacDonald's pace.

MacDonald's stories are very simple and that is why we can be a success. If a storyteller wants line-by-line translation, the tale should be told as simply as possible.

It also depends on taste. If I like a story, I can put the energy into a translation and enjoy sharing the tale. But if I don't care for a story, it is very difficult to do so.

## Difficulties in Translating Personal Stories

*A personal story often lacks the patterning and repetition that make a folktale easy to translate. And the language used can be much more varied and complicated than that of a simple folktale. Masako speaks here of the difficulties in translating a lengthy personal story told by the Texas-born teller, J. G. Pinkerton.*

When J. G. Pinkerton visited Japan, he wanted to share a personal story ... not a folktale. For this translation, J.G. would tell five or six sentences and then pause. Translating a personal story is more difficult than translating a folktale. I wouldn't normally attempt to do this sort of translation, but because I love J. G. and really wanted to portray his storytelling, I did it. I know that J. G. simplified his story to make the translation easier for me. Still, I had to work very hard to reach a translation that would effectively portray his story. All of my body became an "ear" when I translated J. G.'s story. I listened to the tape he sent many times to understand his story. Then I thought, "I have to learn more English to get this."

J. G. had brought me a red cowboy hat. And J. G. always wears a white hat. So I wore my red cowboy hat, too. That made the story event more entertaining, because the hats highlighted the great contrast between us, as J. G. is big and I am tiny.

---

## THE ART OF TRANSLATING
### by Paula Martín

*Paula Martín wowed audiences during the King County Library System StoryFest International in Washington State with her rapid-fire bilingual storytelling. Later I traveled to Cuba with Paula and had the pleasure of her translation for my storytelling. And even later we collaborated on two book translation projects. Here Paula comments on her experiences with these various forms of translation.*

Language is a wonderful thing. It's what defines us as human beings. When a baby is born, the baby's crying is "translated" into words such as "she's hungry" or "he's wet." As the baby grows, the surrounding world gets translated into words ... the child names people and things dear to him.

With words we study, we seduce, we love, or we fight. And when we are gone, words, and most especially our stories, are all that remains from us in our loved ones. Language from this point of view is much more than deciphering words. It's connecting and communicating with our fellow beings; it's an essential part of human nature.

Words have a definition, but they don't hold a single meaning. Words are "alive" and even in the same language do not mean the same to different people. The dictionary may define *lemon* as a citric fruit, but that definition doesn't hold the same emotional meaning for a person drinking cold lemonade on a hot summer day as it does to a person who has just poured lemon juice over an open sore! If words are alive, even more so are stories. The same story told by the same person in a different setting, becomes another story.

So if words and stories are *alive* in their original language, is it possible to translate them into another language?

To be the translator is a great responsibility. I often hear the phrase *"traduttore—tradittore"* (translator—traitor), because of the difficulties in being faithful to the original text, because of the things that could get lost in the transition.

Then there is an eternal fight between "literal" or "free" translation. I think that one has to make a decision regarding the specific use of what is to be translated. In storytelling that goal is to offer an aesthetic, artistic experience. The beauty of language has to show. When translating, one has to say all that is said in the original story, without adding anything that isn't there and to say it in a way that sounds natural and correct in the translated language. Translating involves finding creative and ingenious solutions to many problems. If there are rhymes or leit motiv phrases, they have to "sound" well in the translated language. If I am working on a written translation, I will choose the good-sounding option and will add a footnote if this is not a literal translation. If it is a live performance, I work this out beforehand with the storyteller for whom I am translating. When a phrase or sequence is repeated within the story, after a couple of times I stop translating. As the story unfolds, I leave more and more of the original language in it. At the end of a performance I have people tell me "I felt I could understand Spanish." This is partially so because of all the added ingredients of storytelling.

In storytelling the story is conveyed in much more than words and language. There are gestures, facial expressions, inflections of the voice, differences in the gaze, and all these combined add up to the storytelling experience. All these added ingredients we have learned to translate naturally in our lives. We read body language, we understand facial expressions, we decipher a gaze when somebody is looking in a "special way," and that's translating as well.

The cultural meaning of words could also stand in the way of translation.

For example, the word *liberal* in Spanish stands for a right-wing type of ideology, whereas in English it means exactly the opposite. Languages have different types of energy and different possibilities as well. English, with those beautiful monosyllable words, is a very rhythmic language. Most words have a beat at the end. In Spanish the beat is mostly on the syllable before the last one, so it makes it more like a waltz. In English those beautiful onomatopoeic verbs such as knock, ring, screech, *and* scratch let you do sound effects as you tell. We don't have anything like that in Spanish, but we do have beautiful full open vowels in our words. There's an African story "The Talking Skull" in which a fisherman finds a skull and asks, "What brought you here?" to which the skull answers "words." In Spanish I say, "*la palabra*," and all those big open a's let me open a skull type of mouth that I could never achieve saying "words." English has many sounds; Spanish has many gestures and facial expressions.

When I tell bilingually I redo the actions and the gestures in both languages, phrase by phrase. The most important thing while doing this is to be rhythmic, to tell fluently; the changes need to be seamless. It's not something that you think, "here I cut" or "here I translate." Instead, it's something that you need to let flow, and if you are concentrated and inside the story, it flows. It's like driving a stick-shift car. You listen and feel when the engine needs a shift of gear; it comes with practice. But practice and rhythm are things that we need to achieve in a single-language storytelling as well, so they are not new abilities for a storyteller.

Knowledge of both languages is necessary for the storyteller. I can flow and tell easily in Spanish and English but have a hard time doing the same thing with Spanish and Portuguese. Both of these languages are very similar, and one can understand the other one without mastering the language well. I had a hard time trying to tell in Portuguese. While performing in Brazil, I ended up telling in Spanish and let the other ingredients fill in the "meaning" holes left by the lack of language. When this is the case, and no translation is possible, trust your story and trust your telling, and the story will be conveyed. What remains unknown is completed by the listener.

I remember Kazako Furuya telling epic stories in Japanese, and I could see those gigantic creatures appearing through her tiny self. Likewise, I could perfectly understand Billy Seago's stories even though he told them in sign language.

And there's the beauty of what remains a mystery, unknown, exotic. I love not knowing the exact meaning of the Guaraní *Yasì Yaterè*, the Chinese *Nung Guama*, the Mapuche *Trelque Huecufe*, or the Skagit *Ya how!*

Language is a wonderful thing and translating stories allows us to communicate far beyond our differences, to place ourselves in the most incredible environments, and to recognize ourselves as a single part of a universal puzzle.

*Chapter 7*

# Performing in a Second Language

Several tellers have written of the difficulties of performing in a second language. This chapter presents a reflection by Tokyo teller Masako Sueyoshi about her experience telling at the National Storytelling Festival in Jonesborough, Tennessee. Though Masako has told in English to American and Canadian audiences on many occasions, this event was one to which she gave intensive preparation and much considered thought.

In a second article, Jill Johnson talks about her work telling stories in French in Cameroon. Jill had been a Peace Corps health care worker there years ago. But recently she returned with somewhat rusty French to apply a new skill . . . storytelling.

Neppe Pettersson is a Swedish speaker living in Finland. A small group of Finns happen to be speakers of Swedish as their first language. Thus Neppe tells mostly in her native tongue, Swedish, to other Swedish speakers within Finland. However, she sometimes receives requests to tell for Finnish-speaking audiences. She discusses the problems that doing this presents.

Priscilla Howe shares about her attempts to tell in French in Belgium and her use of friends to help get the colloquialisms right.

---

### PERFORMING THE JAPANESE TALE IN ENGLISH
by Masako Sueyoshi

*Masako Sueyoshi performed at the National Storytelling Festival in Jonesborough, Tennessee, in October 2005. She discusses the difficulties of conveying the essence of a Japanese folktale to an American audience.*

### The Importance of Rhythm

It's difficult to translate the rhythm of the Japanese stories. I decided to say the chants in Japanese so the American audiences could hear the Japanese rhythm. Then I would just tell them in English what the chant had said. But audience participation would be a problem. In "The Treasure Field," for example, the Japanese audiences sang with me on:

> *Hitotsu yama kose, en-yara-ya.*
> *Futatsu yama kose, en-yara-ya.*
> *Mitsu yama kose, en-yara-ya.*
> *Takara-no hara-go aruso na.*

In Jonesborough, I told it double. First I sang in Japanese and then told in English. I said, "Please sing with me when I show my hand" (holds hand out to audience). Just sing:

> *en-yara-ya.*

This is easy for American people.
And also the Old Man's chant, "Don't go! You will die!"
I told it in Japanese:

> *Ikuna Ikuna*
> *Ikeba inochi-wo*
> *Ostusmbe. . . . "*

I wanted American people to hear the Japanese rhythm. This doesn't sound the same in English. So I said it double. Japanese and then English:

> *Ikuna Ikuna*
> *Ikeba inochi-wo*
> *Ostusmbe. . . . "*
> "Don't go!
> You will die!"

American audiences participated with me on the "You will die." I didn't ask them. But even children participated with me without being asked to do so. Because I wanted to show the Japanese rhythm of the song, I chanted in Japanese and after that I told the English double.

### Onomatopoeia

To American people Japanese onomatopoeia is special. So I used onomatopoeia every time. I used it in Japanese. For example,

*"Beloli,"* means "swallow up"
*"Ton ton,"* means "knock knock"

Japanese audiences like Margaret Read MacDonald's English onomato-poeia in the story of "The Little Old Woman Who Hated Housework": "swishety-swishety" and "clickety-clickety." So, I thought American audiences would like Japanese onomatopoeia.

But when I translated MacDonald's stories into Japanese for readers, I changed the American onomatopoeia into Japanese. For example, Little Boy Frog goes "Hop Hop Hop" when told in English, but when I put it in my Japanese translation, I changed it to the Japanese *"Pyon pyon pyon."*

## Preparing the Story Text

After I have done the first translation, I still might need to make changes. It depends on the time and the audience. If they understand the first time, I can tell by their faces.

I have to explain certain cultural differences during the storytelling. For example, Americans are unfamiliar with many Japanese traditions. They don't know about shape-shifting animals such as the *tanuki* (a kind of badger) and magic foxes. Or about *yamamba*, the Japanese witches.

If I don't explain that in the olden times people believed that the *tanuki* was a shape-shifting animal, the audience cannot understand the story.

Many things are different in Japan. The bathroom is different. Grave sites are different. These might require explanation in a story.

I practiced polishing the English many times. During the practice time I found that either I could leave out words to simplify or I needed to add more explanation about Japanese culture.

I told the stories to my English language teachers. They are foreigners. If their faces were puzzled, I added more explanation.

So the translation in English should not be a direct translation from the Japanese. First I translated directly from the Japanese version that I tell. But I found that each story could not work with just that. Then I added words or reconstructed them.

So when I told my stories in Jonesborough, the English story was longer than the Japanese story because I had to add many things to explain Japanese culture and to add double chanting.

## Performing in English versus Japanese

In Jonesborough, I told seven stories in English. I also performed three stories in Japanese, as I wanted the American audience to enjoy my stories totally in Japanese.

When I performed totally in Japanese, Kate McClelland told the story outline first. Kate's translation helped American audiences enjoy my performance. She and I shared the stories from heart to heart to respect each other, and I really appreciated it.

Some people told me they liked my performance best when it was totally in Japanese, because they could hear the flow of the story.

However, I am not only a *performer*. As a *storyteller*, I also wanted to connect with my audience directly through the words, even though my English is not so good. The performance totally in Japanese reminds me of the way you experience story in Kabuki. You read the story in the program first. And then you just watch the performance.

I worked hard so I could tell directly to the audience and make the storyteller's connection.*

---

## TELLING IN A SECOND LANGUAGE
### by Jill Johnson

*Jill Johnson had to revive French language skills from her Peace Corps days when she recently returned to perform in Cameroon. Jill gives useful hints about working up a story in a not-so-familiar language.*

I approach this topic with more than a little trepidation. I am not bilingual like tellers Olga Loya and Leeny Del Seamonds. I do not work side-by-side with native speakers of other languages, as do performers like Margaret Read MacDonald and Fran Stallings. But still, I have successfully told stories and given workshops in a bilingual environment. So, perhaps there are a few things that I can share with tellers who wish to explore this challenging and interesting way to tell. Although I have worked with teller/translators and I have told in other languages, I find that I do not approach the experience in the same way as others do. It seems that each teller working in a bilingual context creates his or her own unique way of dealing with the situation.

### Translators Can Lose the Nuances of the Teller

In October 2004, I was a member of a National Storytelling Network (NSN) storytelling tour to South Africa. As part of our visit, we visited Lesedi Cultural Village, a sort of South African theme park, with recreations of tradi-

*Interview with Masako Sueyoshi, Yanai City, Yamaguchi-ken, November 28, 2005.

tional Xhosa, Zulu, Pedi, and Lesotho villages. At the end of the tour, we were escorted into an open area. Beneath us was hard-packed earth; a fire blazed—a perfect setting for storytelling! Three local women were waiting for us. They had been recruited—somewhat reluctantly—to tell us stories. They began their stories quietly, speaking in their own languages. They seemed embarrassed, afraid perhaps that we Americans wouldn't understand or appreciate their stories. But gradually, they sensed that we were really listening and began to relax. As the soft sounds of their voices carried into the night, I could smell the wood smoke and hear the night sounds. It was easy to imagine them with a group of children at their feet . . . to hear the banter and laughter.

But I found myself getting more and more annoyed at the loud, bombastic delivery of their translators—all men. Even though I couldn't understand the words, I wanted the men to pay attention to the gentle nuances of these stories. I wanted them to translate the stories *as these women told them* — not create their own version. And therein lies the dilemma of bilingual telling: how do we hold on to the authenticity of the tale in the original language while still engaging the English-speaking listeners?

After our South African experience came to an end, I went on to Cameroon in Central West Africa and did a number of workshops and performances there. Fifteen years before, I had lived and worked in Cameroon for two and a half years, and it was wonderful to be back! While in Yaounde, the capital city, I did a number of performances in French. (Cameroon is one of two English-French bilingual countries in the world; the other is Canada.)

## Techniques for Rehearsing in a New Language

The first thing that a teller who tells in another language needs to know is this: you don't have to be a fluent speaker of the language. My French, generally speaking, is terrible. But you DO need to study your story—and the words and phrases of the language—VERY carefully. The process of preparing a story in another language is quite complex. It will make your job much easier if you choose a simple story with few characters, one that you already know well in English.

First, you must be sure that you have a good translation. That means finding a fluent or native speaker of that language to create or review the story and check for problems. There may be outdated words or phrases, language that is no longer used. There may be words or phrases used in some cultures, but not in others. (I once used an idiom widely known in France, but absolutely unintelligible in Cameroon!) Then, you need to rehearse the story with that speaker. You must review—not only pronunciation but also phrasing and emphasis. The language—its rhythm, inflection, resonance, diction—must SOUND right. At this point, you may need to simplify some words or phrases precisely because they do not sound right. The guideline: if you are spending too much time trying to pronounce or say it, change it. Next, the rehearsal part can be really intense, because you must practice and practice this story until the words, phrases, and sentences come almost without thinking; until you can start to actually SEE and FEEL the story happening as you tell (just as you do when you tell in English). Then comes the fun part. Because now, you can begin to play with the language a bit, create impromptu responses that will loosen up your story and your delivery . . . make it come alive. For example, in the French version of a story called "The Elephants and the Bees," I created impromptu responses to the flight of the bees away from a giant forest fire. My script simply says that the bees said, *"LE FEU! LE FEU"* (which means "the fire, the fire!"). But, at various times, I added *"Allons-y!"* ("Let's get out of here!") or *"Vite, vite!"* ("Quick!" or "Hurry up!") and other quick, easy words or phrases. When I first did it, I was stunned at how that simple step helped the story to come alive for ME. And we all know when a story comes alive for a teller, it can create magic for an audience as well.

All this can be difficult and time-consuming. But there are some wonderful benefits to this process as well. Once you have thoroughly mastered the story in the target language, you begin to sense something new, something completely different from the same story in English. You begin to work in the rhythms, the flow of the other language. Let's use "The Elephants and the Bees," the story mentioned previously (found in *Thai Tales: Folk Tales of Thailand* by Supaporn Vathanaprida, Libraries Unlimited, 1994) as an example. In English, the story is a straightforward folktale that builds step by step to a strong climax and then subsides to a much gentler ending. But in French, the story has many more ups and downs and the action is much more volatile—and it's fun! (Now I wonder what differences there are when the story is told in its original language: Thai!)

Another story that I told in Cameroon in French was the classic American Jack tale "Jack and the Robbers." Here, I discovered that the appeal of the story to young Cameroonians was almost exactly the same as to kids in my American audiences. They loved the rhythmic parts of the story (traveling "up and down and up and down" on their knees!), making all the animal sounds (although the Cameroonian kids, perhaps being a bit closer to rural life, showed real fear when I first made the sound of the bull!), and the noisy melee of sounds at the end of the story. I had been warned that Cameroonian audiences probably would not participate as much as I would like, but that turned out to be dead wrong!

## Performing with a Cameroonian Musician in French and English!

On my second trip to Cameroon in 2005, I had a chance to work with a wonderfully talented young musician/storyteller named Zagor. He is a graduate student at the University of Yaounde and a master player of a traditional instrument called an *mvette*. Although our joint appearance had been scheduled months before, we met only days before the performance. But language barriers (both his English and my French are rudimentary) fell away as we rapidly realized our mutual love of telling and performing. As we rehearsed our separate stories, we quickly agreed that we had to do a tandem tale: a traditional Cameroonian folktale in English and French. We choose "The Lion, the Monkey, and the Tortoise," a simple, raucous tale with a universal theme. I shall never forget the delight of those rehearsals: excited shrieks as we discovered yet another comic bit we could use; quiet, intense moments as we debated a point of interpretation. Many times, as I struggled with the language, I remember jumping to my feet and acting out my interpretation until that wonderful "aha" look came over his face. Then, backstage, just before the performance, I had another idea. Why not, just at the climax of the story, reverse the languages? I would speak in French, he in English. With all of our facial expressions, gestures, and movements, much of the meaning of the climax would be clear; so, it wouldn't matter if we mispronounced a few words. Zagor looked at me as if I had gone slightly insane, but he agreed and we brought down the house. God, it was fun!

## Demonstrating the Value of Storytelling
## Brings Respect for Local Tellers

One other benefit of performing in another country can be overstated, but it is there, nonetheless. The presence of you—the foreigner—can help government officials or other potential supporters of storytellers and storytelling from that culture realize the value of their own artists and the art. When I worked with officials at the U.S. Embassy, they were astounded to discover all the talented performers available for cultural events and exchanges. The teachers that I taught in workshops began to realize that they could use local storytellers in their classrooms to help teach a much broader range of subjects and topics than they had previously considered. In a workshop that I presented for the American International Schools of Africa (AISA) annual teachers' convention in Cameroon, I had teachers of all grades and all subjects. In one exercise, we used a typical Cameroonian folktale and demonstrated how it could be used to teach everything from math to music. One of the participants was a University of Yaounde professor of education, who assured me that he would make his future teachers aware of these possibilities. I had more than one Cameroonian government official admit to me, sheepishly, that he didn't know these resources were there!

## Triggering Memories

Days before I left Cameroon, I was in the kitchen with a dear friend. For weeks, Aurelien, a successful businessman and entrepreneur, had politely avoided any discussion about "this storytelling thing." Then, suddenly, softly ... "I've been remembering. . . . " he said, "the stories my mother told . . . , when I was small." Then, he began to sing a lullaby in Yambassa, his own language. I will never forget that moment.

---

## A SWEDISH-SPEAKING FINN
### by Neppe Pettersson

*Neppe Pettersson is a teller from Vasa, Finland. She tells in Swedish . . . her mother tongue (even though she is Finnish). Here Neppe writes of the difficulties of telling in her country's majority language, Finnish.*

My name is Neppe Pettersson. I'm forty-five years old, live in Vasa, Finland, and am a full-time storyteller, probably the only one in this country. I belong to a shrinking minority of Finns with Swedish as our first language (only 6 percent of the population). We have got schools, newspapers, television, and so on in the Swedish language—but we are not from Sweden; we cheer for the Finnish ice hockey team, as we are Finnish.

I'm a trained kindergarten teacher (Finland Swedish college), I have been working for eighteen years with children's programming (in Finland Swedish television), and I do most of my storytelling work in Swedish in Finland. I'm able to work in Swedish in Scandinavia, as Swedish, Danish, and Norwegian are fairly similar to each other.

## A Swedish-Speaking Teller Tackles Telling in Finnish

Occasionally I do storytelling in Finnish, but Finnish is not my mother tongue. I'm fluent enough in Finnish, but my vocabulary is not as wide as in Swedish. I don't know very many sayings in Finnish and I haven't got the poetic sense of language in Finnish. So the stories I tell in Finnish become much poorer in language.

If I want to tell stories in Finnish, I have to accept that the level of my spoken language will never be the same as for one that has it as this mother tongue. I can make the stories flow dramatically as well as in Swedish, but I can't expect anything more than that from myself.

To work a story into Finnish, I start with taking a story that I know well. Then I just tell it out loud to myself. I try not to "chicken out." When I stumble on a word that I'm not sure about, I try to "talk myself around it" and use other ways of putting the words to tell the same thing. I have to find the flow of the story right from the very beginning to see whether the story accepts to be put into Finnish in my mouth.

When I have gotten to "The end," I can then go back and look up the correct words and phrases, and make notes of them. Then it's back to tell the story out loud for a second time, now trying to incorporate the words I hadn't known before. Then I'll keep on telling the story until it has a good flow and I do not stumble on any words I don't know. It's still not very rich in language, but the telling has gotten life and soul.

### Searching for Poetic Language

Once I found the story of "Shingebiss and the North Wind" on the Internet. In that version there is a song that I tried to put into Finnish. But it didn't sound very good. So I called my mother, who is fully bilingual, to get her advice. "Well, how about using this or this instead?" She masters the poetic words, and if I need them, I have to go to a person whose first language is Finnish; I just can't make it up or look it up.

### Selecting Tales for Translation

I prefer to use fairly "simple" stories to tell in Finnish. And with simple I mean, for instance, personal stories, legends or ghost stories, stories using everyday language. The next level is folktales such as fairy tales. But I will never work myself up to tell *Kalevala* in Finnish. *Kalevala* is the Finnish national epic, originally sung in Finnish. I retell the stories in Swedish very often, but *Kalevala* is almost "sacred" in Finnish. One ought not to stumble on *Kalevala* (unless you are using that as humor on purpose).

### Honesty About Linguistic Skills

Two years ago I did not take any paid gigs in Finnish, but now I do. I like to tell my employers "what they are buying," and if they accept my poor language (but great storytelling!) then we've got a deal!

I'm working on my storytelling in English at the same time. I remember the first time I had to tell *ex tempore* in English. It was at a festival in Stockholm, Sweden, with a lot of famous foreign storytellers. "Everyone has to tell something tonight!" Oops . . . I took one of my sure-fire stories, about the Finnish noodle heads. But it was a disaster . . . I found myself making all beginner's mistakes that anyone can imagine . . . (I really hope no one remembers anything from that evening).

*Recently Neppe sent me a happy email: Since I wrote about my telling in Finnish I have developed it much more :-) This summer I have been working as a guide at an outdoor museum and have had mostly Finnish-speaking visitors. This has made my Finnish much more fluent and secure, and I have also started telling more stories in Finnish.*

## PUTTING STORIES INTO FRENCH
## FOR AUDIENCES IN BELGIUM
by Priscilla Howe

*Priscilla Howe tells of her attempts to find just the right phrase for telling in French. Fortunately, she had friends who could help!*

### Telling in French

I've been traveling to Belgium every two years to perform, mostly in English, but I do have one school where I perform only in French, and I sometimes have public performances in French. I majored in French in college and lived in Belgium in my junior year in 1981–1982. Even with that background, I find it a great challenge each time, and each time I learn more. The friends I stay with have two children (now in high school). I began telling stories just to these children. I would watch their reactions, watch for that puzzled look that meant I'd gotten something wrong. I'd ask for alternate phrases when it was clear I'd said something that didn't quite work. The children and their parents (who speak English well) would coach me. I'd listen to the way the children retold the stories—that's how I learned that the expression I was using for "black eye" wasn't the common one. Early on, I realized that I didn't know the tense used in stories, the *passe simple*, which is rarely used in regular speech, usually just in literature. My friends suggested I tell in the present tense, so that is what I do.

I think in French—I'm not translating each thought—but I don't have the nuance of the language at times. Before I perform, I practice with my Belgian friends. I make sure I know any unusual words, repetitive phrases, and songs within the stories perfectly. Once I was working on "Sir Gawain and the Loathly Lady" with my friend Marie, who warned me about a phrase that can be misinterpreted to be quite vulgar. That averted a little chaos with a high school class! Occasionally I'll forget a word when I'm performing. In that case, I either talk around it or ask the listeners, who are well aware that I am not speaking my native language. Once I couldn't remember the word for the lid of the washing machine. The fourth and fifth graders helped me out the first time (*le couvercle*), and then the next time it came up in the story, they were ready to call it out. L'Institut St. Louis is an inner-city school where most of the kids are from other countries, so French often is not their native language either.

When I perform in French, or for ESL kids, I choose stories that have a strong physical component, so the listeners can understand quite a bit from my body language, voice, and gestures. As I do in English, I use puppets in between stories—my puppets also speak French. I choose stories that do not depend on wordplay or on American cultural references.

## Crowd Control

One challenge is energy management. When I'm performing in English, I'm able to pull in listeners who might be drifting slightly, with just a word or a gentle look. When I'm performing in French, I'm using so much of my energy to keep the story going, I don't have quite the same control. This makes it particularly difficult with the youngest children (*les tout petits*, as the teachers call them). Then again, it might just be that Belgian kids, especially at this school, don't have the experience of listening to a storyteller or even being in an audience.

## Stretching U.S. Listeners with a Tale in Another Language

Here in the United States, I also sometimes perform in French or Bulgarian (the other foreign language in which I'm fluent) in one specific way. Usually I tell "The Ghost with the One Black Eye," and then I announce that I'll tell it again, in another language. I give the audience the choice of language. This story has a repetitive physical action and phrases, and each character is quite distinct, so the listeners understand it completely and they join in. I tell them the three reasons I do this: (1) so they understand that telling a story is more than just saying the words, (2) so they know that they could learn a foreign language, and (3) because it's big fun for me.

## Chapter 8

# Story in Language Instruction

To aid in language instruction, a simple tale can highlight specific words from the language to be learned. We see this possible usage in Chapter Three in the texts for "Grandfather Bear Is Hungry" ("I am SOOO hungry") and "Little Boy Frog and Little Boy Snake" ("Hop hop hop hop" "Slide slide slide slide"). Or a simple tale told in a second language can be repeated, encouraging the students to join in, until nearly the entire story can be told by the students in their second language.

Here Nat and Jen Whitman describe their dual-language performance with Mandarin teachers in Hong Kong. Judith Wynhausen notes the use of nursery rhymes with Russian children, Michael Harvey talks of using Welsh within inner city schools in Cardiff, Jill Johnson mentions her work in a French language camp, and Julia Klein presents two multilingual programs being used in Premen, Germany.

---

### MABELA THE CLEVER IN HONG KONG
by Nat and Jen Whitman

*Here a sample story shows how Mandarin vocabulary for audience participation was inserted into a story performance.*

We tell stories in tandem and often perform for student assemblies at Hong Kong International School where we work as teachers. Last year we began a conversation with the Mandarin teachers in our school about how to integrate Mandarin into these storytelling assemblies. We were fortunate to have two colleagues, Georgina Guang and Lillian Wei, who were eager to explore the possibilities of bilingual storytelling with us.

For our first attempt at bilingual storytelling, we selected a folktale with key vocabulary that the students were already working on in their Mandarin classes. We chose *Mabela the Clever* (Margaret Read MacDonald, illus. Tim Coffey, Albert Whitman, 2001). It's a story of a small mouse that outwits a cat. We gave Lillian and Georgina the written text of the story, and they wrote a line-by-line Mandarin translation to become familiar with the language. At first, they used their written translation as a script, but as we spent more time exploring the story together, they decided to put the paper down and to just play with the story in Mandarin.

We spent many afternoons working out different ways to present the story bilingually. We finally settled on a story theater approach using language partners. Georgina and Jen were the mouse and Lillian and Nat were the cat. Nat/Jen would tell a part of the story in English and then Lillian/ Georgina would tell key phrases in Mandarin. Lillian and Georgina were selective in their telling so that they translated only what was integral to the plot. An important aspect of this experience was that Lillian and Georgina weren't just acting as "translators"; they were telling the story *with* us. We were creating the story experience together.

When it came time to tell the story at the assembly, Lillian and Georgina led a few minutes of Mandarin instruction to learn/review the key words that the children would be hearing throughout the tale. The children practiced the phrases *"Tīng"* ("Listen"), *"Kàn"* ("Look") *"Xiǎo xīn shuō huà!"* ("Speak carefully"), and *"Pǎo de kuài!"* ("Run fast"). When these words popped up during the story, we paused for the entire audience to say them with us. Before we began telling, we also practiced singing a song that is repeated many times in the story. When we taught the song, we sang it once in English for the children to understand the meaning, but then Lillian and Georgina taught the words in Mandarin and the children practiced singing it only in Mandarin. When it came time to sing, we sang the song in Mandarin, not English. Lillian and Georgina had worked hard to translate the song in a way that would keep the rhythm similar to the version we sang in English.

The story was a huge success. For several weeks after the assembly we heard children singing the refrain throughout the halls, *"Xiàng qián zou, Xiàng qián zǒu, Bú yào huí tóu, Māo jiù zài nǐ de hòu miàn, hòu miàn!"* Not only was the telling useful from an instructional perspective, it was also wonderful for the kids to see the English teachers and the Mandarin teachers working together. We were certainly sold on the value of bilingual storytelling, and now the four of us can shape a bilingual telling in an afternoon. We've also learned from our own experience that language instruction through storytelling works ... we remember the Mandarin key words in *Mabela* to this day!

Here is the text of *Mabela* as it was used to teach the stressed Mandarin vocabulary. In our assembly performance, the entire story was told both in

Mandarin and in English, but the children all joined in on the phrases shown here.

*Mabela the Clever*: Based on a Limba Folktale

Retold from the picture book *Mabela the Clever* by Margaret Read Mac-Donald. (Albert Whitman, 2001).

In the early times some were clever and some were foolish.
The Cat was one of the clever ones.
The Mice were mostly foolish.
But one little mouse was not so foolish.
Her name was Mabela, and her father had taught her cleverness.
Her father always told her,
   "Mabela, when you are out and about,
   keep your ears open and LISTEN. *Tīng!*

   Mabela, when you are out and about,
   keep your eyes open and LOOK AROUND YOU. *Kàn!*

   Mabela, when you are speaking . . .
   Pay attention to what you are SAYING. *Xiǎo xīn shuō huà!*

   And Mabela, if you ever have to move . . .
   Move FAST." *Pǎo de kuài!*

One day the Cat came to the mouse village and said,
   "Dear mice, I come to offer a special invitation.
   It has been decided that the MICE may join the secret CAT SO-CIETY.
The mice were VERY excited to hear this.
   "We get to join the Cat Club! We get to join the Cat Club!"
   "Come to my house on Monday morning and you will learn all the secrets of the cat."
Monday morning bright and early, the mice were all there.
   "Oh, my, you have ALL arrived!
   How delicious . . . I mean, how *delightful*."
   "You must all line up in a very straight line.
   And you must all learn the secret Cat Society song.
   The song goes like this . . .
   When we are marching,
   we NEVER look back.
   The cat is at the end.
Fo Feng!
   FO FENG!"

*Xiàng qián zǒu, Xiàng qián zǒu,* [Go forward, go forward.]
*Bú yào huí tóu,* [Don't look back.]
*Māo jiù zài nǐ de hòu miàn,* [The cat is right at your back.]
*hòu miàn!* [At the back!]

[This is sung once in English before the story starts. During the telling the song is used only in Mandarin. The onomatopoeic Limba phrase "Fo Feng" is replaced in the Mandarin version.]

The little mice all shouted loudly on the last "FO FENG!"
The Cat lined them up in a straight line.
Mabela got to march in front, because she was cleverest of them all.
At the end came the . . . Cat!
"Remember," called the Cat. "Never ever look back!"
Off they started. Mabela was leading the way so proudly.

*Xiàng qián zǒu, Xiàng qián zǒu,*
*Bú yào huí tóu,*
*Māo jiù zài nǐ de hòu miàn,*
*hòu miàn!*

*Xiàng qián zǒu, Xiàng qián zǒu,*
*Bú yào huí tóu,*
*Māo jiù zài nǐ de hòu miàn,*
*hòu miàn!*

Every time the mice would shout *hòu miàn!* the Cat would grab the last mouse in line.

*Xiàng qián zǒu, Xiàng qián zǒu,*
*Bú yào huí tóu,*
*Māo jiù zài nǐ de hòu miàn,*
*hòu miàn!*

Suddenly Mabela remembered what.
her father had told her,
      "Mabela, when you are out and about
      Keep your ears open and LISTEN!"      *Tīng*

Mabela stopped singing for a moment and listened.
She did not hear a long line of mice singing behind her.
She heard a FEW mice singing.
She heard the Cat's voice getting closer each time they sang!

Then Mabela remembered something else her father always said,
    "Mabela, when you are out and about
    Keep your eyes open and LOOK AROUND YOU."     *Kàn*

Mabela dared not turn around.
But she turned her head just a little to the left.
Just a little to the right.
She did NOT see a long line of mice.
She saw a SHORT line of mice and the CAT VERY CLOSE!

Then she remembered that her father had said,
    "Mabela, when you are speaking.
    Pay attention to what you are SAYING!"     *Xiǎo xīn shuō huà*

She listened to her song.
    "The cat is at the end? What does THAT mean?
    No one is watching the CAT!"

Mabela turned around just in time
The cat had just caught the mouse behind Mabela!
Now Mabela remembered the LAST thing her father had told her.
    "Mabela, if you ever have to move.
    MOVE FAST!"     *Pǎo de kuài*

Mabela DOVE into the bushes . . . so fast . . . so fast . . .
that the Cat pounced on nothing but thin air.

Mabela lived to tell this story.
She told it to her children and her children's children.
Limba parents are STILL telling this story to their children.

It is good to remember the things Mabela's father taught her.
    "When you are out and about, Keep your ears open and
        LISTEN.     *Tīng*
    When you are out and about, Keep your eyes open and
        LOOK AROUND YOU!     *Kàn*
    When you are talking . . . pay attention to what you are
        SAYING.     *Xiǎo xīn shuō huà*
    And . . . If you ever have to move. Move FAST!"     *Pǎo de kuài*

## MOTHER GOOSE AND REPEATED LANGUAGE
by Judith Wynhausen

*Judith Wynhausen finds her "Mother Goose" performances of simple tales based on traditional nursery rhymes are useful with ESL children. She tells here of her use of simple songs and rhymes when telling to children in Russia.*

When I was telling to children who were learning English in Russia four years ago, I tried to repeat certain phrases as often as possible . . . in different contexts if it made sense. I also used my entire body to mime the meaning of the story . . . more than I do when I normally tell. When I tell as Mother Goose, I always invite the children to join in with me to recite the nursery rhymes. With the Russian children we would recite the rhymes several times (as opposed to once or twice for American children) until they felt more comfortable saying them with me. I sang nursery rhyme songs, inviting them to sing along, adding finger movements and gestures. The songs could also be repeated several times.

One favorite with the children was "Who Stole the Cookies from the Cookie Jar?" and another was the song and game "The Hokey Pokey." Both use repetition with small changes that keep the interest up.

## FIRST LANGUAGE TELLING WITH MIDDLE SCHOOL ESL STUDENTS
by Michael Harvey

*Michael Harvey has found interesting ways to introduce Welsh to speakers of other languages. Here are some excerpts revealing Michael's thoughts on this topic.*

I'm starting to do work with year 6 (10–11 years) kids in English medium schools in Welsh and having a ball. I prime them with the outline of the story and a gesture "map" and use pictures as well to avoid English in the telling. Then I talk about the stories, in Welsh, afterwards.*

*Excerpted from Michael Wilson,"'The Story Was Sufficient': A Profile of Michael Harvey, Storyteller," *Cyfrwng: Media Wales Journal*, Vol. 1, April 2004.

I'm working in inner city schools in Cardiff. They are multilingual environments and that is very much about creating a culture within the room. And when I worked in Ninian Park, they were very keen for me to work with kids and with the language support teachers to do work in their home languages. So we've done work in Somali and Bengali and Gujarati, which is great. And what's nice is that there's no big deal. It's just that these kids play creatively using the models that we've done. When I first did this, I wanted everyone to have the experience, so what we did—this was with a Year 5 group in Ninian Park—was write something in Welsh and the kids loved it. I took in something the kids had done in the Welsh medium school, and vaguely told them what it was about. But it wasn't a translation. And then I read it to them a couple of times, put it on the board, and I just got them, as a group, to decide which were their favorite words, rubbed out all the others, then we made a verse based on these words that they just liked the noise of. Then we worked with the vocabulary and structures we already had to put something together. And it was lovely.

So there's that kind of freedom that's offered. But at the same time there's a sense of connection. Whereas if I came from a particular cultural language community, say I was of Somali descent, and I spoke Somali and I went in to work with Somali kids, that would be more like what I'm doing with the English kids. It wouldn't just be about linguistic freedom.

---

## STORYTELLING IN LANGUAGE CAMP
by Jill Johnson

*Whidbey Island storyteller Jill Johnson, tells of using her French tales in language camps.*

One venue I found for presenting tales in other languages (which is really fun) is foreign language camps and classes. The Northwest Language Academy, located right where I live on Whidbey Island in Washington State, provides summer camp experiences for kids ages seven to fourteen in Japanese, French, and Spanish and an English camp for Asian students.* Last year, I was a codirector of the French camp. Our theme was "The Heart of Africa," and we used African folktales extensively in our camp activities. Before the session began, we selected several African folktales, translated them into French, and created dialogue for some of the animal characters

---

*For more information about the Northwest Language Academy, visit www.nwlanguageacademy
.com or call 360–914-0391.

in the stories. In the opening sessions, we had several of the junior counselors present two very simple (and hilarious!) folktales in French. This jazzed the campers and was great fun for the junior counselors as well. Then, we introduced the tale we would all work on for the session. Every camper had a part, and the session ended with the kids performing the tale—in French—complete with drums, costuming, and dancing!

---

## IN EVERY LANGUAGE THERE ARE STORIES TO BE TOLD: MULTILINGUAL STORYTELLING IN BREMEN

by Julia Klein, translation by Leslie Strickland

*Here Julia Klein tells of the innovative uses of story in Bremen's immigrant communities in Germany. Success has been found in using tellers to share stories in both Turkish and Russian in kindergarten and primary classes. And community storytelling events have been able to draw together families from many linguistic backgrounds.*

People from a hundred different countries live in Bremen, the city I've been exploring as a storyteller since 2002. There are neighborhoods in Bremen today in which over fifty languages are spoken. What a treasure trove of languages! What a wonderful opportunity to hear stories in their original languages that I know only in translation.

Since the spring of 2005 I have been organizing multilingual storytelling events in Bremen. These events take place in two different kinds of settings. The one is pedagogical, a storytelling workshop in kindergartens and primary schools that supports the learning of language skills; and the other is cultural, an exchange of stories among families in their different languages. Both projects are described below.

### Bilingual Narration as a Pedagogical Approach

#### The Storytelling Workshop

Bremen is contributing three projects to a nationwide program entitled Support for Children and Youth of Immigrant Background (*FoerMig*). One of these projects is the Storytelling Workshop, which, from fall 2004 to fall 2007, is experimenting with storytelling as a means of increasing language skills for bilingual children. Teachers from seven kindergartens and six primary schools, the Minister of Education in Bremen, the Teachers' Continuing Education Institute (LIS), and the University of Bremen are all partners in this project. The project's research director is Professor Dr. Johannes Merkel, University of Bremen.

Storytelling events are held on a regular basis in the participating kindergartens and schools. Embedded in the stories told to the children are various grammatical stumbling blocks typical for learning German as a second language. Each storytelling session practices and builds on the previously learned grammatical structures. The children in the program are in their last year of kindergarten or in the first three years of primary school, that is, five to nine years old. The percentage of children with an immigrant background in the participating schools and kindergartens ranges from 50 percent to 90 percent. Incorporating the diversity of the languages represented here seems an obvious choice.

## Bilingual Storytelling Events in Kindergartens and Primary Schools

In May 2005 we introduced our bilingual storytelling program together with two women students from the University of Bremen, one from a Turkish and one from a Russian immigrant background.

These narrative events all follow the same pattern: The storyteller visits a kindergarten or primary school class in which some of the children speak either Russian or Turkish. She introduces herself and explains that she will tell a story in two languages. She asks the children who among them can speak Russian or Turkish, and then she asks all the other children to listen very carefully and to pay close attention to her facial expressions and gestures. She proceeds to tell the story in Russian or Turkish.

Each story is told using much gesturing and clear facial expressions. And each story also includes recurring elements, for instance, a song sung repeatedly or a rhyme illustrated with big gestures. These repeated elements invite all the children to join in. At the end of the Turkish or Russian language story, the non-Turkish- or non-Russian-speaking children have a chance to share what they've understood of the story. They tell us what they think the story is about and which words sounded familiar to them. With the assistance of the children who understand the language in which the story was narrated, the storyteller then tells the story once again, but this time in German. She uses the same clear gestures and repetitive, come-join-in elements. Whenever the situation allows, the children then act out the story. In addition, for each story, we've prepared various painting, writing, or handicraft projects that develop the story and grammar themes further and can be done either immediately after the storytelling or at a later time.

The stories are all traditional ones from Russia or Turkey, individually chosen by the student storytellers themselves. We felt it important for the storytellers to have a particular connection to the stories they would be telling.

On the basis of thirty such storytelling events, we have made the following observations. Through storytelling in their own languages, even children who otherwise seldom speak up in class are inspired and encouraged to participate in the storytelling. Sometimes they comment on the story in Russian or Turkish or translate individual words for their classmates as the story is being told. In some of the children it was easy to see their pride in their special knowledge. They eagerly enjoyed helping with the German translation.

Contrary to initial fears of the classroom teachers, the non-Turkish- and non-Russian-speaking children also listened to the story raptly. The decisive element here in holding their attention is the high proportion of gesture and repetition in the telling. Again and again we also observed how the non-Turkish- or non-Russian-speaking children would look in amazement at their Turkish or Russian classmates participating so eagerly in the narration.

The children were clearly overjoyed to have their mother tongue suddenly used in a German institution—far from an everyday occurrence—and were very curious to learn more about the storyteller's roots and her current living situation.

### Fairytales Open Doors: Multilingual Storytelling Afternoons for Families

The idea for multilingual storytelling afternoons arose in a conversation with Sabine Michaelis, a staff member of Bremen's Social Services Ministry. The central question under discussion was this: what form of cultural offering is best suited to reach out to people of highly different backgrounds in so-called flash point neighborhoods?

In collaboration with a well-established cultural center in Bremen, we held the first multilingual storytelling afternoon in June 2005. In preparation for this, we had held a workshop with four women of different cultural backgrounds in storytelling techniques. The event took place in a circus tent set up in the multicultural neighborhood of Osterholz-Tenever. The storytellers related stories from Iran, India, Russia, and Turkey. Throughout the narration I added short summaries in German. We used retrospective and previewing techniques and very clear gestures here too to facilitate understanding. Music played an important role in the narration as well. Two musicians from the City of Bremen Immigrant Orchestra accompanied the fairy tales with instruments and compositions from the country in question. Following the telling of these four stories, the audience was invited to join in a collective storytelling. In five different languages, we then told the story of the stubborn carrot that refuses to get pulled out of the ground. At the end we asked the audience to join in and help us out.

Everyone who could count "one, two, three" in a language that was not yet represented was invited on stage to join the line. At the first event "one, two, three" was counted in twenty different languages.

We have since held two further storytelling afternoons, and hopefully many more are to follow. Our experience to date has shown that this form of event attracts people who otherwise seldom attend cultural events. Following the storytelling on stage, people stayed for a long time to talk and share more stories and play more music at each of these events. Stories invite other stories out of hiding. The particular charm of these events lies in enabling various different languages to be heard, so that each person in the audience will experience sometimes being able to understand more of the story and at other times less. All the different tones unite into a wonderful polyphony in celebration of the language treasures right here in the middle of Bremen.

*Chapter 9*

# Presenting Tellers of Other Languages

The world is drawing closer nowadays and our communities may house wonderful storytellers who speak languages other than that of our audiences. Don't be afraid to invite these folks to your storytelling events. Audiences love the intimate contact with individuals they would not otherwise get to experience. And the human heart finds ways to connect across language barriers. This chapter contains comments from both producers and listeners.

## NURTURING TELLERS WITH HALTING ENGLISH SKILLS
### by Margaret Read MacDonald

When helping to produce the King County Library System's StoryFest International in Washington State, I wanted to invite tellers from cultures our audiences might not have experienced. This meant crossing the language barrier at times.

An hour of work with tellers who are a bit unsure of their English turned out to be invaluable in correcting pronunciations and clarifying confusing story bits. This small investment of time can make the difference between a stunning performance and a confused audience. When the Indonesian artist/storyteller Suyadi came to tell at our StoryFest, I was surprised to discover that he had trouble telling his stories in English. He sketches while telling in Indonesian and moves rapidly. And he is perfectly fluent in English. But combining the drawing with the English telling proved a block. So we took an afternoon off to go to a library with a chalkboard and work through the stories. His festival performances went off beautifully. But he needed that little help to make it happen.

When Kazako Furuya peformed at our festival, she had worked hard to develop a short repertoire of English language children's stories for her library performances. She wanted a little help with pronunciation and that was all she needed. But for her main stage performances, Kazako had decided just to give the gist of her lovely epic singing with *biwa* accompaniment. She performed them entirely in Japanese. A wise choice, as the beauty of her Japanese language performance affected us all. There would have been no way to convey this in English.

Roberto Carlos Ramos speaks no English (or very little). He came to us accompanied by the teller Livia de Almeida, who translated for him. Livia sat or stood quietly at one side of the performance space and translated rapidly as Roberto Carlos performed. She was unassuming and really "not there" to many audience members. One father at my library talked to me a few years later about that wonderful Brazilian storyteller. When I mentioned that he had been telling through a translator, the father begged to differ with me. "I was there," he told me firmly. "That man was telling the stories in English!" Such is the value of a good translator.

But if the tellers available to you have no English at all, and no teller-translator to accompany them, present them anyway. Find someone who speaks both languages to do the translation. Suggest the line-for-line translation technique. Yet if this does not work or seems too cumbersome, just let the translator do a summary before the tale. Fran Stallings and her Japanese friend Hiroko Fujita have made this technique work beautifully in performances for all ages from preschool through seniors. (You can read about their work in Chapter Four).

The important thing is to bring these tellers to your audiences and let them connect. As programmers your job is to seek these tellers out, nurture them into confidence, and bring them to your audience. For years I worked as a fellow librarian alongside Supaporn Vathanaprida. After Su and I had published a collection of Thai folktales, Su began to receive invitations to tell stories at local museums. She always said yes . . . and then told me that "we" were going to be telling stories on such and such a date. I encouraged her to tell the stories herself . . . they were tales from her grandmother and her homeland. She preferred to simply talk about the Thai culture and then introduce me as the storyteller. But when she joined Toastmasters, Su had to learn a story. This was my chance. I coached her and coached her. And then I put her on the program for the Seattle Storytellers' Guild Tellabration. I took her to the performance site well before the event and stood her onstage. We hit her with lights. We miked her and had her run through her story. So when her time came she was confident. And of course . . . she was hooked. Now she tells for school assemblies and wherever she is invited. But without this nurturing, her talent might have gone unseen.

When presenting tellers with no experience speaking to groups, it is best to provide them first with small, intimate audiences. A few years ago the Seattle Storytellers' Guild and the Washington State Folklife Council collaborated to produce two Traditional Tellers weekends. We set the events at Fort Worden State Park, where we could rent former officers' homes. We invited four traditional storytellers and asked each to tell stories in the living rooms of these old houses. Their audiences were twenty-five folks sitting on sofas, chairs, and on the floor at their feet. Though several of these tellers had not told stories to such groups before, the intimate setting made it comfortable for them to share their stories. Some of them felt at ease later telling stories in schools and libraries and even in stage settings. The trick is to bring your teller to new audiences gently and to prep your audiences for this new listening experience. At the Fort Worden Traditional Tellers weekends, the opening sessions each day gave listening hints to participants, so that they would approach the traditional tellers with respect and understanding.

---

## LISTENING IN ANOTHER LANGUAGE

*Here are comments by audience members who responded to hearing tales told in languages they did not speak.*

### A Student's Response to Fujita-san

*Regina Ress sent the comments of her student Kat Redniss, who had seen Hiroko Fujita perform in Japanese in collaboration with Fran Stallings.*

I was extremely moved by the simple beauty and power of the stories, and the impressive collaboration of these two wonderful women, Hiroko Fujita and Fran Stallings. I had not known what to expect from the performance, especially in regards to the approach with language, but the entire afternoon communicated effectively the passion and pride with which Fujita tells her stories. What also came across to me was the deep reverence with which Fran Stallings has approached these stories and the process of being a helping voice.

On Sunday, April 9, 2006, Fran Stallings and Hiroko Fujita told Japanese folktales and stories to a lively audience. Present was a mix of New York

University students, many of the faces from our storytelling class, as well as several families with children ranging in age from a few months old to ten or eleven. The two storytellers began the afternoon by playing with traditional Japanese toys while audience members filed into their seats. This created an interest and showed a playful side present in both women. This activity also created a relaxed, informal atmosphere in which the audience began to feel at ease to ask questions, participate, and enjoy themselves.

The performance was formatted so Ms. Stallings would introduce the stories, telling some history behind the tales, which helped to expose us, the spectators, to aspects of Japanese culture and past. One particular instance was in describing the traditional Japanese food, which helped us to understand both customs of Japan and the twists of the story. Stallings would give a brief description of the action of the story, because it was to be performed in Japanese. She mainly established the characters and the bare bones plot of the piece. Often, she would leave the ending a mystery and Fujita would show us the ending. I was impressed with this for a number of reasons. First, we as an audience were then able to predict what we thought was going to happen. The children and adults were excited and drawn in, waiting to see whether they had correctly predicted the ending of the tale. Most memorably, the tale of the two greedy snakes that end up devouring each other stands out. Fujita's physicality made the ending of the story so clear that no further clarification was needed. Because there were small children in the audience, Stallings would frequently ask, "So what happened?" allowing them to tell their version of the story and to make sure they did understand what had gone on.

Both storytellers maintained a magnificent engagement with the audience. They were warm, open, and quite gracious in their recounting of the stories. Fujita has a brilliant command of prop use. What moved me the most was the simplicity of her props. She needed no fancy puppets or elaborate snakes. She used her own body and simple household objects to create a wonderful spectacle of movement and intrigue. Her movements were also simple, very clear, and easy to interpret. Frequently she used repetitive movements and asked us to move with her, not only bringing us into the story but also teaching us skills or cultural games.

What was most amazing was the language. Fujita speaks beautifully and uses a wide variety of voice techniques. I thought prior to viewing this piece, how will we participate without knowing the language? Her use of repetition served as clarification and I felt that any participation was welcome and safe. I was not afraid to say the wrong words. I am glad, however, that I bought the two small publications containing her stories. Looking over them, I can appreciate the difference between live storytelling and a story that exists on the page. Listening and reading give me completely different reactions to the story. Not being able to understand the language helped me to realize that we as humans communicate any way we know how, through gestures, voice, demonstration, and so on. Stories are universal.

This beautiful performance showed me the ultimate power and importance of storytelling. Not only was I able to learn several stories, but I also learned about culture, history, and humanity.

## An Italian Performs for a Castellano-Speaking Audience

*Paula Martín shares her experience in an audience of Spanish-speaking Porteños listening to a visiting Italian teller.*

We in Buenos Aires are always searching for "the story," the story that is special, new, different. Last April we had the pleasure of having Roberto Anglisani, an Italian storyteller, student of Marco Baleani, performing at our Argentine Book Fair and storyteller's conference. And to that very literary audience he told . . . for one and a half hours . . . in *Italian*, to about 500 adults . . . "The Ugly Duckling." He had us all hanging from a thin hair. We all felt the poor ugly duckling and then we all felt as swans. I know we all knew the story, but the way it was told was just so incredibly beautiful that we just couldn't stop listening. That's when I realized that it really wasn't "the story" . . . but the way it is told . . . and the way a person can "express" him or herself. The job then is not to find "the story" to tell . . . but the "true teller" that is within ourselves.*

## Listening to Cristina Taqeulim's Portuguese Telling

*Regina Ress tells of her experience with a Portuguese teller.*

It can be thrilling for an audience to watch a teller performing in a foreign language. If enough of the bare bones of the story is known or given, the telling then becomes a delicious immersion in language, culture, and imagination. I remember seeing the great Portuguese storyteller Cristina Taquelim tell the story of Tía Miseria. Because I know the basic story and have some background in Spanish and French, I followed most of her Portuguese with excitement. I felt as though we had both crossed a tightrope together.

*From StoryTell posting, September 26, 1999.

## LOST AND FOUND IN TRANSLATION:
## THE STORY TELLS IT ALL
by Kevin Cordi

*Kevin Cordi hosted Fran Stallings and Fujita-san at his California high school. He writes here of his enjoyment of their telling style.*

To translate, one must have a style of his own, for otherwise the translation will have no rhythm or nuance, which come from the process of artistically thinking through and molding the sentences; they cannot be reconstituted by piecemeal imitation.
> —Paul Goodman (1911–1972), American author, poet, and critic

As I hung up the phone with Fran Stallings, I couldn't believe what I'd agreed to do. As a recent hire at Hanford High School, I had just begun developing a storytelling program and couldn't believe that I had just booked two storytellers to come to my school—a high school that had not been kind to performers in the past. I had not only agreed to a public performance in our theater but also to a day of workshops. To top it off, Fran told me Fujita-san did not speak any English and would tell only in Japanese. Needless to say, I was worried. Our students were not accustomed to public performances and were definite strangers to audience etiquette. How would I convince high school teenagers that this elder had much to share if she spoke only Japanese? Fran assured me that she would translate, but my experience with translation had not been pleasant.

My school, located in the Central Valley in California, consisted of over 60 percent Latino students, many from migrant families. My experience with translation was when a bilingual "specialist" would come in to parent meetings and translate for the parent. With my limited knowledge of Spanish, I remember wondering whether the parent would receive my messages accurately through the translator. I always believed the system had marred any real attempts of communication. In best-case scenarios the teenager would speak as a mediator for the translator. When messages would fly back and forth, excluding me, I always felt as though I had to force myself into the conversation to say something, but when it was said, miscommunication followed. Suffice it to say I was weary after my phone call with Fran. I didn't want this experience to mirror the parent meetings. How was Fran going to help bridge this gap? My experience with translation was more like Bill Murray's in the movie *Lost in Translation*, when he would simply nod his head and walk around lost. Instead I wanted to know how best to help my students find the beauty in the language of the storyteller and translator's work.

When the day finally arrived, I immediately noticed the presence Fran and Hiroko Fujita-san both had in telling a story. To my surprise, Fran did not interpret each word; she helped only when Fujita-san needed additional clarity. In the morning when they conducted workshops together, Fran simply echoed the understanding. Fujita-san moved with expert skill, sharing handmade Japanese woodcrafts. When Fujita-san didn't understand something, she simply worked with Fran until she knew. Fran continued to assist her by explaining nuances in language and even in many cases physically demonstrating what she did not understand. They worked in concert. My students asked a barrage of questions while Fran and Fujita-san performed stories. These young people took a vested interest in sharing their culture and discovering more about Japan.

The real testament, however, was in the performance. I admired how Fran began with a vignette of the story that Fujita-san was about to tell. She expertly showed a picture of the story, and then Fujita-san would tell it with expressive physical reactions and eloquent Japanese. At one point I watched with intrigue when Fran told about a bridge and then displayed a wooden handmade bridge to the surprise of the audience. This conveyed just the right amount of vision and words so that we could see the whole story. We were captured by the majesty of Fujita-san's telling, rich with detail and body movement. This helped us see the images.

To me, the telling tone came as the lunch bell rang midway into the story. Normally hundreds of students would bound out of their chairs and run for the exits to munch down hamburgers and drink Cokes. But that day was different. Not one student stirred from the chairs, because Fujita-san and Fran told their story in such a commanding way that every one of the students had to hear the story's end.

First, weigh your words, then speak openly.

— India proverb

Or

The language in which we are speaking is his before it is mine.

— James Joyce

This experience has never left my memory, and as it happens, many years later I received my chance to tell. On a Fulbright scholarship in Japan, because I was a storytelling teacher, I was asked to tell for an elementary class in rural Japan. Naturally I was nervous but I practiced the telling with a translator. One of the stories was "The Great White Mug" written by Barbara Freeman, first told to me by Dr. Flora Joy. This story is physical. I pour water down my shirt with the telling and encourage audience participation. As I began telling with my translator, Harumi Osaki, I was uneasy,

I was not sure when to stop, but as I worked with my partner, she would not only translate my words but also my expression and my body language. Soon the children were recalling the story with me, and when I poured water down my shirt we celebrated in the laughter. Afterward, the kids hugged the translator and me. We were connected to the story and were telling together.

> As a tiger may lose its footing on soft ground, so people may be tripped up by sweet words.
>
> —Chinese proverb

As a result of telling this story and telling for other schools and communities, I was chosen out of a delegation of 200 Americans to address the farewell banquet before we returned to America. Many were in attendance, including one of the greatest Kabuki artists in the world, the mayor of Seki, people who had survived Hiroshima, and the special guest, the vice minister of Japan. I was honored to be the keynote speaker but also frightened of the experience. Because the speech was in the evening, I wanted to begin by saying "Good evening, friend," which is *Konban wa tomodachi.*

I practiced and practiced, but when I came to the microphone and saw the vice minister, I said "cowabunga." The room fell silent. Instead of saying "Good evening, friend," I had greeted the vice minister and the rest of the delegation just like Bart Simpson and the Teenage Ninja Mutant Turtles. Silence. We needed to laugh. I was able to present the rest of my speech with more comfort and was later complimented on the speech by the vice minister himself. In the end, even though the words were not exactly right, I was told the heart of it was. I guess I was not so "lost in translation." We simply enjoyed our mistakes and were able to communicate the universal language of laughter, which needs no translation.

Initially I had no concept of how translation can help add to the telling of a story. However, after witnessing it and performing with a translator, I can see how the right words are important but not as essential as the right connection. It takes time, practice, and, in some cases, laughter. But all the work is worth it. Telling with a translator helps kids find new discoveries in telling and learning with stories.

## PRESENTING ANA GARCIA CASTELLANO
## IN NEW YORK CITY
by Regina Ress

*Regina Ress produces a storytelling series in New York City. She tells here of presenting a teller from Madrid, who spoke only in Spanish. Ress writes "clearly words are only one of the 'languages' of story-telling."*

Ana Garcia Castellano is a storyteller from Madrid who travels around Spain, Europe, Africa, and Latin America. We were in a festival together in Rio de Janeiro where I saw her perform her best-known piece, *Stories and Songs from Don Quixote.* I invited her to bring it to the storytelling series I produce in New York City. As Ana is a highly expressive and very physical teller, I knew that language would be no barrier.

I introduced each story in English, setting the tone and giving key plot highlights and occasional Spanish words for the audience to listen for. The performance became a weaving together of my introductions and Ana's telling. The audience was delighted. We did the same thing for a folktale program for schools in Connecticut and New Jersey. The children were very excited that they were able not only to "get" what she was saying but also to participate in the telling. Ana and I are developing a program we can do together, bouncing the English and Spanish stories and languages back and forth.

## CROSS-LANGUAGE TELLING IN EUROPE
by Tim Sheppard

*Tim Sheppard's Storytelling FAQ tries to keep a finger on the pulse of international storytelling. Here are his reflections on storytelling-in-translation and producing tellers in languages not understood by the audience.*

### Subtitled Events

In France there is a lot of support for the arts, and the government heavily sponsors big storytelling festivals. Although I have not been to any, some British tellers have been and reported back. At least one big festival offers simultaneous translation in three languages. This is done with good resources and technology, where, out of sight, translators put the words onto screens. The screen is large, above or at the back of the stage. This technique is also used for major conferences and operas.

The advantage is that one can look at the storyteller and get all the nuances of intonation, gesture, and expression, while still reading the words to get the meaning, hardly moving the eyes. Obviously it's not perfect, having a split in the attention, but it's about as good as it could be. The only thing better would be to have a skilled storyteller/translator do the same thing but into individual earpieces worn by the audience. This, too, is done in big conferences, but the translators don't have to have skills of artistic expression!

## Bardic Tellers Whose Power Crosses the Language Gap

I have heard many tellers in foreign languages, at Beyond the Border, the Wales International Storytelling Festival. There they have almost no resources available for technical solutions, but it hasn't stopped me from enjoying the tellers. These tellers, who are mainly in the bardic traditions of various long-established cultures, have a power and presence that no other storyteller comes close to. They also use rhythmic chanting, trance, gesture, and monotonous music, which powerfully draw the audience in, whether they understand or not.

Beyond the Border uses two strategies—giving a translated summary of the story either before the performance or interspersed in sections within it. Often Ben Haggarty takes this on—he is the festival codirector, is a skilled teller, and has often visited where the foreign teller lives and takes an interest in individual techniques and traditions. Of course Ben can't translate directly and still needs the help of translators or discussions in broken English in order to understand the story. Other times, and of course for interspersed translation, a translator is needed —but he or she rarely has storytelling skills. However, this doesn't always matter; the power and expression come through the teller, and the translator simply reveals the meanings, much like the screens in France do.

## Key Gestures/Words

The Pandvani singers, including Ritu Verma, from Madhya Pradesh, India, use a sophisticated language of ritual gesture in their telling. This is very helpful because if the story is summarized at the beginning, the audience can spot during the performance, through the gestures, what part of the story is being told. This year we had a skilled Indian dancer/storyteller,

Megan Lloyd (actually native Welsh, but trained in Indian dance), demonstrating the gestures as the summary was told at the beginning, enabling the audience better to spot the gestures later. This principle could very usefully be extended to words, too. A translator could, during the prestory translation, speak the foreign words or phrases for key objects, actions, and characters, so that when those sounds were heard in the performance, the audience could recognize them and orient themselves to the plot.

## Listening in Another Language Not Always a Barrier to Enjoyment

A year or two ago I saw an excellent teller, Mimi Bartholemy, from Haiti, now living in France. She knew enough English to translate her own stories but still told some of them in French. And I'm glad she did. Her language and accent were wondrous. My French is very rusty and was never fluent, and I'd not come across her particular dialect and accent, which were very different from standard French. Yet, her expression of words was crystal clear—enunciated so well and in fact delivered as if each syllable were a tasty morsel of some fine delicacy that she had to enjoy in her mouth before releasing it—that I had no problem following her stories. Her joy that oozed out of every moment was so delightful and infectious that I was fully involved and fascinated, getting the entire emotional journey of the story.

I think this is an important thing to realize, for festival directors and audiences who are unused to foreign languages. Listening to foreign language performance is not necessarily a problem! It does restrict some understanding, but doesn't necessarily prevent it. It doesn't prevent the telling from being mesmerizing. By actually listening, much can be gained from a telling in a completely unknown language, and quite a lot of word meaning can be gleaned if the language is another European one, because the words are related.

On one occasion in Belgium I was in the audience for a gala show celebrating the opening of a circus school. Much of the excellent show was of physical skills. But when a Flemish comedian came on, I groaned to myself. I didn't know a word of Flemish. Neither could I easily get out from my seat, squashed in the middle of a crowd. However, to my great surprise, as I listened to the comedian, I started laughing at all the jokes until I was thoroughly enjoying the show. I still didn't understand a word of it! But the comedian's skill and timing were excellent, and his art of making people laugh effectively worked beyond language, though I was probably the only one there who realized that. It is often quoted that 93 percent of the meaning we get from oral communication comes from other than the words; that is, the gestures, facial expressions, intonation, timing, and the like. I can well believe it, after having laughed at apparently nothing for half an hour.

And it wasn't just entertainment I gained— I learned a lot that night. I think the same applies to listening to storytelling in a language you don't know.

---

## TIPS FOR ORGANIZING STORYTELLING THROUGH TRANSLATION
### by Murti Bunanta

*Dr. Murti Bunanta organizes biannual storytelling festivals in Ja-karta and organizes storytelling tours to various sites throughout Indonesia. She often presents visiting tellers from other countries and has given serious consideration as to how best to use these folks who do not speak the language of her audiences.*

As a person who was born in a country with speakers of approximately 800 regional languages, most of whom also communicate through a national language, it is not a strange experience to listen to stories in languages other than your own. Therefore, I am confident in organizing storytelling programs through translation. I established the Society for the Advancement of Children's Literature (SACL) in 1987, a nonprofit organization that pioneers activities to develop children's reading in Indonesia. Since 1989 we have invited many storytellers from England, Japan, the United States, Singapore, and Malaysia. And I am convinced that this works.

But it is important to consider certain concerns seriously in order to make these events a success. The producers or the organizers themselves should be persons who have a passion for stories, are knowledgeable about what storytelling is all about, and enjoy the events themselves. So this event is not a job for just any event organizer who happens to be good at organizing other events, such as weddings, birthday parties, and seminars. I emphasize these concerns because ignoring them has caused problems here and it could happen anywhere.

Other important concerns are the plans and preparations. Are you organizing a public event or a school event? An event for a special audience: children in orphanages, older citizens, children at hospitals, adults? These choices affect the response of the audience, which influences the choice of which storyteller to invite. Consider how well you know him or her. What is the character of his or her stories? Humorous or touching? Energetic or calm?

A producer should also be able to imagine in advance what is going to happen with the event. This is important regarding not only the site but also most importantly the preparation and cooperation between the story-tellers and the producer. Stories should be discussed and sent in advance to allow the translating storyteller to translate and get to know, understand, and learn the stories. If the invited storyteller doesn't cooperate well and has not sent the stories ahead of time, or if there is not enough time to rehearse, then the translating storyteller has to be prepared to make improvisation during the performance. A translating storyteller is not just a translator but a translator who is also a storyteller. The person who teams up with the guest storyteller needs to be someone who also likes to tell stories.

I want to stress that it would be much better if the translator were also a storyteller or at least a trained amateur. Since SACL has grown into a prominent organization with a number of trained volunteers, it has helped me to figure out and decide in advance which volunteer is the best to team up with a particular storyteller. A storyteller may need different translators depending on the color and character of each story the teller performs. If there are songs and chants, an appropriate partner is needed. It is worth noting that long stories with long sentences should be avoided because it makes the pace slower and lessens the tension of the story.

I also want to emphasize that the contribution and the role of the translating storytellers should also be appreciated. They make the story appear and reach the audience. Without translation there is no story, no matter how good the invited teller is, because the audience then sees only gestures and actions but doesn't get any story. This is even worse if the story doesn't require much audience participation.

However, I am convinced that storytelling through translation can be well received by audiences who don't speak the teller's language, providing that necessary preparations, concessions, and plans have been made. Besides, a story that is performed in two languages is unique, because you feel as though you master a language other than your own and at the same time you learn the beautiful sound of the other language. Leaving the event, the audience will feel enriched not only by the story but also by the language. And by bringing in a skillful teller who doesn't speak the language of the listeners, you will also improve the skill and the experience of the local tellers.

### Comment by Margaret Read MacDonald

*Murti makes some interesting points here. She has a large cadre of well-trained storytellers who can work translating English tellers into Bahasa Indonesia during her events. She makes a conscious effort to match the personalities of her translating tellers to those of her guest performers. And she even considers the particular stories we tellers plan to perform when selecting the translators she assigns us. I should also mention that a rapport between teller and translating teller helps enormously. She has paired me often with the inimitable teller Suyadi. And she often assigns Agus Rahman to translate for my more lively tales, because he and I both love to jump around the stage and play off of each other. For one of my quieter stories, she may assign Ariyani Djatmiko or Tety Elida or Devina Erlita Farahsari, quieter female tellers with good audience-communication skills.*

*Her comments about the credit due to the translating tellers are very important. These are co-performers . . . not mere translators. And they deserve as much praise as the teller being translated.*
*Murti also alludes to the fact that her tellers learn during their acts of translating the stories of visiting tellers. By "dancing" with the visiting teller, so to speak, they experience unique pacing, language usages, and audience-communication techniques. It is a way of walking in another teller's shoes for the space of a story. I am reminded of the Balinese dance instruction technique in which the teacher places the child's body in the proper position for each move. By allowing the child's body to "feel" the position, the child learns. In somewhat the same way, Murti's translating teller gets to "feel" the visiting teller's story.*

---

## WORLD LANGUAGE STORY TIME AT THE KING COUNTY LIBRARY SYSTEM

by Maren Ostergaard

*At the King County Library System, an effort is being made to create storytellers who can work in various languages. Here librarian Maren Ostergaard tells how new storytellers are trained. These folks are reading picture books aloud for the most part, though some may choose to tell stories as well.*

We are working in our libraries to create quality services for our immigrant populations. One thing we want to do is increase the number of trained bilingual people who can conduct story times in our libraries. The King County Library System offers story times in many languages. Since the fall of 2003, we have offered 6 trainings and currently have almost 100 trained individuals in our database of World Language Story Time providers. Currently we have trained providers to present story times in Spanish, Russian, Albanian, Cambodian, Arabic, Chinese, Farsi, French, German,

Hebrew, Hindi, Urdu, Japanese, Korean, Polish, Russian, Ukrainian, Slovakian, Somali, Swahili, and Vietnamese.

This training is required for anyone who wishes to become a story time presenter in our libraries. Although we cannot pay individuals to attend the training, the training is FREE and offers them essential learning and skill practice. This training provides attendees with ideas, tools, techniques, and inspiration to create quality story time presentations. Upon successful completion of the training, attendees are added to a list of story time presenters that our libraries can contract with for their story times. Libraries will pay $40 per story time.

What does a contract World Language Story Time presenter do?

- Select appropriate story time materials (support provided by the community children's librarian).
- Prepare and present the story time in his or her language or bilingually, as arranged by the library.
- Connect story time attendees with the community library staff.

Because World Language Story Time providers will be working with young children, they must undergo a Washington State Patrol background check.

The training is called *Story Time Success: What's Behind the Magic.* It is a full day (eight hours) of training. In addition, we can offer it for STARS credit, if individuals are interested. We also periodically offer half-day trainings for current World Language Story Time presenters to share thoughts and ideas.

Here is an overview of the training:

What goes into an effective story time? Why do we do story times? How is it done? Come to this workshop to learn what's behind the magic—how to connect children with libraries and literature through successful story times.

*Learning outcomes:* As a result of this training, participants should be better able to:

- Explore and describe why story times are a core part of public library service.
- Identify the key elements of an effective story time.
- Select and use developmentally appropriate, culturally relevant stories and activities in story times.
- Use at least three methods to introduce language and literature in a story time.
- Identify and integrate activities that support emergent literacy skills.

- Evaluate the developmental level of an audience and use one to three strategies to modify a plan, as needed.
- Demonstrate how to share a book with a group of children.

Once an individual has completed the training, the person's name goes into a database of trained providers that is shared with the children's librarians. It is then up to the branch staff to hire for the programming that best suits their communities' needs. World Language Story Time presenters can be hired to present story times bilingually or completely in their home language. The presenters can indicate which libraries or which regions they would be willing to offer story times in. The program has been very successful.

---

## THE BABEL BYPASS
by Ben Haggarty

*Ben Haggarty speaks here of the manner in which he presents epic singers from various cultures. His aim is to showcase their telling in their own languages.*

My work as a producer of international storytelling events in Britain, has often involved presenting fabulous storytellers who were working in languages unfamiliar to their audience. However, on these occasions the nature of both the storytellers and the audience has been rather specific, as has been the objective.

When staging any event, the first consideration must be for the audience: what are we putting on, for whom, and why? Those performers that I've presented, who have had little or no English, have in almost all cases been *epic singers*—often the direct equivalents of European professional storytelling traditions whose existence is remembered by such titles as *bard*, *minstrel*, and *troubadour*. It is important to be clear that the majority of the audiences before whom these performances took place were thoroughly familiar with the world of stories and storytelling. The audiences were thus already somewhat specialized, and I mentally categorize these events as "storytellers' storytelling," rather than "public entertainment." The focus of the events lay clearly in the demonstration of performance techniques and in allowing the unhindered flow of performance energies, rather than in any attempt to convey a detailed sense of story, language, and meaning. We wanted to inspire the audience with a general impression of the artist's commitment to, and relationship with, his or her work, rather than try to communicate the stories in depth. These were therefore projects examining "form" rather than "content" (though, of course, "content" gives rise to "form"). My colleagues and I have presented Kyrgyz "Manaschis," Central Indian "Pandvani" singers, Turkish "Asiks," Kazakh "Akyns," Manding "Djelis," Bangladeshi "Palagan" performers, and more—all genuine bearers of highly evolved, *formal*, "professional" performative traditions.

Our strategy for presenting most of these performances was based on a simple "mediation" by English-speaking performance storytellers. Our English-speaking performers worked for some time in advance with the visiting performers using interpreters and, occasionally, academics to understand the essence of the story, the tradition, and the style. The presenters were then free to present contextual information and the stories in a précised form, before each performance, deploying all their skills as professional communicators comfortable on a stage. If the performance style had any clear gestural indicators, the English-speaking tellers physically referenced these, too, so that the audience might roughly locate themselves in the progression of the narrative. I should however re-emphasize that in such presentations word-for-word translation was never the aim. These were to be encounters with living performance forms, and it was enough to give the audience an abbreviated sense of what the emotional progression of the stories might be. Our overriding aim was to demonstrate how most of these epic-singing traditions had evolved for formal public presentation in a time before electronic amplification rendered the need for certain performance adrenalines redundant. Our prime objective was to give our specialist audience a sense of the flow of energy generated by epic performance traditions. We wanted our audiences to witness how the energies demanded by the formal telling of epic and myth, before large numbers of people, push the performer (to a greater or lesser degree) into an altered state of consciousness.

My experience of presenting foreign language storytelling has therefore been mainly limited to promoting performances by very dynamic, stylized epic singers; I have rarely attempted to present foreign language performances derived from the more casual or informal "fireside" storytelling traditions, or from revival storytellers whose medium is primarily spoken prose. I have witnessed several attempts to do this by other promoters in Britain and also abroad, and I feel that it presents almost insurmountable problems for a nonspecialist, public audience. The truth is that, after a fairly short amount of time, no matter how inspired the performer's language is, no matter how wonderful the content of the tale, unless a prose teller is doing something *extra*ordinary with his or her vocal technique or physical bearing and gesture, a foreign language experienced as speech alone, becomes for the nonspecialist, an *excluding* Babel, and boredom sets in through lack of involvement. This means the performance has to be translated, but how?

I've attended storytelling events in Israel that tried simultaneous translation through headsets; I've attended public events in Paris where exact translation was projected as subtitles; and I've listened many times, in many countries, to halting events with the (nonstoryteller) translator interrupting the flow of the guest storyteller (and the dramatic flow of the story). I've even been given a piece of paper to read. None of these approaches has been very satisfactory at the basic level of entertainment—though all have interested the specialist in me. If we are devising events for the *general public*, it is inappropriate for us to impose our personal academic preferences upon them.

The rare public presentations of this nature I've witnessed, which have been both accessible and entertaining, have all involved bilingual performance storytellers (rather than translators) interpreting for fellow performance tellers. These events have taken the form of thrilling, live, and improvised tandem tellings—but their success has been due to the play of exceptional experience and stagecraft, and a proficient mastery of two languages. Perhaps the most famous demonstration of this was by Dario Fo in the tours of his *"Mistero Buffo"* storytelling shows in the early 1980s. Even though he was a fluent English (and French) speaker, he chose to tell in Italian with actor interpreters, who became his comic foils. The chances of finding such chemistries are rare.

In predominantly English-speaking Britain, the promotion of international storytelling has benefited from the ubiquity of our mother tongue as a favored second language for many nations. We have enjoyed many European, Arabic, African, and South Asian language-speaking storytellers, telling in more or less fluent English. Their bilingualism has meant they can delicately pepper their tellings with choice phrases from their mother tongues, bringing to the experience exhilarating glimpses of unknown wider worlds and helping us to trust them as authentic guides.

By contrast, an utterly exasperating experience is the bilingual storyteller who pedantically insists upon translating every word of his or her own material, line by line, or paragraph by paragraph, effectively telling the story twice. At best such storytellers are making a political point about the preservation of a minority language (at worst, they are simply showing off their language mastery). Here the story, and its play with the audience, is all too easily obstructed by an agenda adopted by the storyteller that has no intrinsic connection with the inner content of the tale. Such events need to be signposted as "language lessons."

The truth is that bilingual storytellers are relatively rare. So how are we to respond to the challenge of presenting prose storytellers to audiences that don't have access to their language? As a promoter I know many fine storytellers—for example, in France—whom, being solely French speakers, I cannot justify promoting in Britain (just as they couldn't justify promoting me there). Perhaps we should turn to tradition itself and see what it suggests?

I find that, after some consideration, the storyteller's traditional response to the crisis caused by the barriers of Babel, comes to mind . . . and it is provocative. Hah! Truly, the trickster is the storyteller's god!

Let us consider "Monsieur X," a gifted French-speaking prose performance storyteller. Perhaps we should just accept that British audiences will never get to meet Monsieur X' in person; however, they could meet his taste for stories. As tellers of traditional tales, it is hubris to pretend anything other than that *we do not own our stories*. Whom did our common and unknown ancestors evolve these stories for? The response "exclusively for we and our kind (be it nation, family, clan or cult) cannot be uttered with any confidence. I would suggest that the vast majority of traditional tales that speak to us do so because they resonate with our sense of belonging to a common humanity with a far greater common experience of life and death on this planet than some would have us believe.

I would therefore humbly propose, at the risk of controversy, that the contemporary storyteller's most honest response to the dilemma of Babel's barriers might best be decided on the grounds of what would most benefit the audience and the intention of the unknown ancestors. I would suggest that contemporary storytellers should *do what has always been done*: they should—with the help of translators, shared conversation, and dialogue, and with honor and respect—try to understand the traditional tale that Monsieur X happens to tell. They should then return alone with it—a new story—eased from one mother tongue into another, added to their repertoire for the delight of their own audience. They should then pass it on, to the best of their ability, with as much relish and freedom as possible, deploying all their skills as they see fit, in service of the tale, perhaps acknowledging Monsieur X . . . but perhaps even not. They should be free to let the story take fresh roots and be born anew in themselves and in others.

If this results in a seamless cultural *translocation*, then so much the better! Of course, there may be gains and losses, but the essence of a story—worthy of being classed as traditional—is able to exist and voyage at a level far deeper than the separating superficialities of language and the seductive poetry of words. I believe the "ancestral voice" wants to be heard, and it will help as many other voices as it can to speak on its behalf— in all the Babel tongues of the world. Something of value will pass through everyone who attempts to tell a tale well and who tries not to stand in front of it.

*Chapter 10*

# Presenting Workshops Abroad

## Margaret Read MacDonald

I have been asked how I do workshops when working abroad, often via a translator. I wrote a short piece about this for *Storytelling Magazine* a few years ago. This chapter contains some of the advice I gave then.

### PROBLEM ONE: CONVINCING THE ORGANIZERS TO LET YOU USE TRANSLATION

See the advice in Chapter Two on general translation problems. When presenting a workshop you face some additional problems. It may be difficult to convince the producers of the event that you want simultaneous (i.e., line-for-line) translation. The producer is usually an English speaker, likely a superior to the participants . . . their boss, professor, or a highly respected organizer. This individual often believes that these underlings need to *learn* to understand English. Listening to you talk will be *good* for them. Even if they don't quite get it all, they need to *try*.

Because I have come all the way from the United States at great physical and monetary expense (a lot of my bilingual work is pro bono), I want to actually *teach* these folks how to tell stories. So I insist that they be able to understand everything I am saying. This means I need to be translated.

At a library association workshop in Alor Setar, Malaysia, the organizer insisted that everyone understood English perfectly. I doubted this would be the case. Sure enough, all but five of the participants did understand English quite well enough to follow my workshop. But the worried faces of those five let me know that they weren't really getting it. Fortunately a friend who had translated for me previously was attending the workshop. I made a plea to the organizer to let me use translation and she nodded reluctantly. Suraya jumped up and began to translate on the spot for both my stories and those of Jen and Nat Whitman, the tandem tellers working with me that day. So the five Bahasa Melayu–speaking librarians got the full benefit of the workshop after all.

It is difficult to deal with this sort of English-language superiority attitude of many organizers. Because they have worked hard to earn their own English language competency, they feel others should be able to fall in line behind them. So it is necessary to be somewhat delicate in not hurting their feelings, while gently insisting that we want translation "just to make sure everything is really clear." You might point out that hearing the story twice . . . in English AND in the local language . . . helps with English learning for everyone.

## PROBLEM TWO: FINDING A TRANSLATOR

Usually a dinner is planned for the night before the event, and there is a chance to meet some of the other players in this event. I try to spot someone with a good energy that would match mine. Then I attempt to convince the organizer that I should use *that* person to translate for me. If I can convince both the organizer and my spotted "translator" that this is a good idea, I try to find a half hour to show the intended translator what I have in mind and let that person experience my pacing. The results are not perfect. But they are far better than the alternative . . . leaving half of the audience wondering what on earth you are talking about!

Of course, with luck you will be invited by a *storyteller* . . . and this person can translate in a flowing storytelling style . . . allowing you to do the sort of tandem telling I describe in Chapter Three.

## PROBLEM THREE: PLANNING AHEAD

It is usually possible nowadays to email your handouts to the producers so that they can have English language copies available for the participants. Sometimes you can convince the host country organizer to get a few of your stories translated into the local language. This is a lot of work for them. You can stress the value of having the story in both English and the local language. This has many benefits: It allows the participants to be absolutely clear on the translation of the English. It also improves their own English to see the two texts side-by-side. And it allows them to use the story in either language when they do their own tellings later. It is also useful should they try to teach the story to their own students or fellow teachers.

Bring copies of your handouts with you. It is surprising how often handout items . . . or entire handout sets . . . are not available at the sites when you arrive. And often the organizers can't even find them on their computers, even though I have a paper trail showing they were sent. I usually bring along a hard copy and an electronic copy.

Materials such as paper and photocopy budgets are not easy for some organizers. So I try to keep my handouts to a minimum and always use front and back to save paper. I often rewrite my stories to make them briefer and clearer for folks who do not use English as a first language, and this shortens the handout, too.

Try to get a copy of the publicity for your workshop ahead of time so you can understand why they *think* you are coming and who they *think* you are!

Get into the room well ahead of the participants and rearrange the furniture to suit your needs. Be proactive about this. Yes, those big tables *can* be moved to the side. No you do *not* want to stand behind a lectern. Some things are not movable, though. Each stage in Thailand features a set of small tables at one side with a photo of the king, and objects of veneration. These cannot be moved. But such culture-sensitive objects are usually obvious.

Clarify exactly who will be bringing you to the workshop site . . . .and exactly when and where the pickup will be. This sounds so simple—but is not always so. In Kuching I waited on the hotel steps as directed for an hour one morning until I finally called the Sarawak State Library to ask about my pickup. No one had been assigned to come for me, and no one was paying any attention to the folks sitting quietly in the conference room awaiting my arrival. When they did fetch me, I was simply shown the room and left alone with the patient participants: library workers from outlying areas who were thrilled to have been flown in for this workshop . . . but were way too intimidated by the big city folks to query why the workshop leader was not there.

If there is something you need to keep yourself comfortable, plan for this ahead of time. Always bring bottled water with you. One site will have it in abundance . . . the next will not even have any in the building. And you usually don't want to rely on tap water. Keeping yourself healthy is important. Find out where the bathroom is first off. And bring lots of Kleenex to use there. Have an alternative activity in mind to occupy the class should you be called to the loo on an emergency.

I remember one telling in Sabah when my daughter, Jen Whitman, and her husband, Nat, had eaten a bit too much local cuisine the night before. I told the first story that day and they were to follow. But I looked up to see that Nat was missing from the room. So I told another story. Then I saw that Nat was back in his seat but Jen was missing. Eventually they both were in the room at the same time, so I introduced them, and they told a very quick story before both disappeared again! It does help to have two

sets of tellers on hand for these emergencies! You can carry various reme-
dies with you, but I suggest taking acidophilus tablets throughout any trip
as a useful prophylactic.

## PROBLEM FOUR: CULTURAL SENSITIVITY

Try to find out about the culture in which you are working. Ask friends
about common errors made by foreigners. My Thai friend, Wajuppa Tossa,
jokes about an American student who was the laughing stock of the graduate students. He had walked up to a girl at a party, put out his hand, and
said, "Hi! My name is John Watts. What is *your* name?" Such *rude* behavior
amazed everyone. You never walk up to a Thai person and just blurt out
your name like that. Instead, it is polite to enter the conversation gently
and after a while work around to subtly discovering facts about each other.

In Thailand I must not point with my finger or foot. I must not touch
anyone on the top of the head. I must not place myself higher than a person
older or more deserving of respect than myself. I must never touch a monk,
as I am a woman.

When working in Islamic cultures, I must not hand anything to anyone
with my left hand. I either remove dogs and pigs from my stories, or suggest
that the participants substitute more suitable animals when practicing the
stories I am teaching. My daughter, Jen, laughs about their telling in Alor
Setar, Malaysia. They had launched into their version of "The Squeaky
Door." I was watching from the rear of the room when I suddenly realized
that they were about to put a PIG into bed with Little Boy. I began to
quietly but frantically make chicken wing–flapping motions in the back of
the room. Jen peered at me most curiously and then finally grinned . . . just
in time to put a CHICKEN into the bed. Whew!

Don't jump to conclusions about your audience. The first time I began
a workshop for an audience of Malaysian women, I was taken aback by the
head coverings and long skirts. They seemed so covered up. "Oh, my! How
will I ever get them to "jiggety-jog" with me?" I thought. No problem! A
more participatory and enthusiastic audience I have never seen! Likewise
my Japanese friends thought it would be impossible for Masako and me to
get the 1,000-strong audience of Japanese ladies (and a few men) to stand
up and dance with us during our "Cockroach Party" rendition. No problem! Up they jumped and danced as well as any audience.

## PROBLEM FIVE: DELIVERING THE WORKSHOP

Here is an example of my "Playing with Story" workshop. This offers hands-
on teaching of audience-participation folktales. This is my favorite work-

shop and the one I use most when meeting new groups . . . especially when those are beginning tellers.

You will, of course, have your own workshop material and format. But perhaps it will be useful to see what has been happening with mine.

## Introductions First

### Myself to Them.

Based on whatever the publicity stated about myself and the workshop, I try to give participants a clearer idea of what they are in for. I attempt to do whatever the publicity *said* I would do. Problems can be avoided by clear communication in the emails beforehand, but sometimes you arrive to see yourself billed in an unexpected way.

### Them to Me.

It is important to find out who your participants are before you begin. Chatting as they assemble in the room helps with this. A quick around the room introduction is useful. Often they don't know each other, and this helps them feel more comfortable when you ask them to work together. You may be in for some surprises. At one Sarawak workshop, I was alarmed to discover that many of the participants did not work with children. And many who did work with children offered only craft programs, not using many picture books and never telling stories. A few seemed confused as to why on earth they were at the workshop, though a free trip to Kuching, the country's capital, seemed to figure large in this. I changed my plan for that two-day workshop. I introduced some of the stories I had meant to use, but also spent a half day talking about picture book use and a half day helping them shape their own stories. Many had heard folktales from family members and wanted to know how to preserve these.

Always bring materials with you to offer alternative workshops. Bring along various tale texts and workshop outlines for emergency changes. Expect nothing. Be flexible. Go with the flow.

## First Activity

### A Surefire Audience-Participation Folktale.

"Jack and the Robbers" is my favorite. I tell the story, encouraging much audience participation. This is often the first time the audience has experienced anything like this, but I keep after them until all are taking part and having a good time. Well, all except that lady in the back row who looks so awfully pained. I know how she feels, so I leave her be for the time being.

I then go over the story structure. I replay the text. Stopping to talk about the parts . . . noting the repetition . . . the changes in mood . . . the little riff "Up the hill and down the hill and through the valley." I note the importance of openings and closings for any story . . . the pause to gather the audience before the first line . . . the closing silent moment.

I break the class into groups of three and send them to stand in small circles, insisting that they do stand for this exercise. With some cultures it takes a lot of cajoling to get them all on their feet facing each other ready to tell. I emphasize the importance of using the whole body when learning a story. I also talk about eye contact . . . and the importance of being good audience members for each other. They may need a few moments to get to know each other before they begin the storytelling.

One teller in each group now begins the story. I repeat the tale's first line, shout, "Begin!" and clap my hands. The individual who has agreed to be first teller now begins telling the story just heard to his or her group. The group has been instructed to participate with the teller in the chants and songs. After a while I clap my hands and shout, "Pass it on!" The second teller now picks up the story right where the first teller stopped. And so the story passes around and around the circle as I clap (or ring a bell) to signal passing time.

As the groups finish, I hand out story texts for the tale they just learned. These are usually in English. I encourage the participants to do the telling exercise in whatever language feels most comfortable. So, for example, in Kota Kinabalu at the Sabah State Library workshops, we have groups telling in Bahasa Melayu, Mandarin, Kadazan Dusun, and English. I allow time for the participants to make notes on their texts, adding words and phrases in the language in which they plan to actually tell the story. If the texts are provided only in English this is important. It is useful for them to work in small language groups to find the best ways to translate the English chants and phrases into Kadazan Dusun, Bahasa Melayu, and Mandarin. I often ask individual groups to then share their translation decisions with the whole class. This can be time consuming, but makes sure that the participants have a story text that is going to work effectively for them. Often one small group of participants will come up with an unusually delightful idea for translating the story . . . and others will write that down to use, too.

If time allows, I follow this story learning by calling six students to the front of the class. I ask the person on the left to begin telling the story . . . then pass it down the line every time I clap. This allows the experience of telling in front of an audience . . . without having to stand up alone for a whole story. It also reveals the many delightfully different ways one story can be interpreted. If there is time, it is fun and useful to have everyone in the class participate in this exercise . . . six or so at a time.

## A Tandem Tale

### Next: A Tandem Tale.

I tell a story with two main characters and then talk about the story structure. Then I bring up an eager-looking class member to act the tale out with me in story-theater fashion. I talk about this technique, in which we each tell the story while acting it out. The voice of the teller is never to be dropped. Thus Grandfather Bear says: "Grandfather Bear came out of his cave. He said, 'I am SOOO hungry!'" We act this out and tell at the same time. After a demo of this technique, the participants choose partners and rehearse the story. If there is time they can tell the story twice, switching roles. And, of course, if there is lots of time it can be fun to have a couple of teams demonstrate for the entire group. In some cultures this is expected and seems to provide great enjoyment for the group. In others it seems embarrassing for the participants. When finished, everyone gets a copy of the tale text. And again they need to tailor it to their own language needs.

### Mini-lecture.

I talk about "how to learn a story" and "how to perform a story." I base this mini-lecture on information in my *Storyteller's Start-up Book*, but I created a handout in very simple English for overseas use.

## Break Time

Make notes of things people ask about during the break. You can address your answers to the entire class later.

## A Simple Audience-Participation Folktale

After the break I teach a story with lots of repetition and simple English. "The Squeaky Door" is excellent for this. I can use this story to demonstrate another technique . . . that of bringing audience members up to participate in a story. I bring up a little boy . . . cat . . . dog . . . pig (or chicken . . . goat) . . . horse . . . as Granny tucks each in.

## Bibliography

I share a simple bibliography of storytelling resources useful to beginning storytellers. Theses are available on Amazon.com, even overseas. In many of the areas I visit, personal resources are severely limited. So I try to make sure the handouts have all of the tale texts I have used as well as good information to get participants started telling. This may be all the printed matter about storytelling they ever get their hands on.

## Questions

Make a time for questions. You can also address various questions that came from individuals during the break. If one person was puzzled, likely more were too.

## Last Story: Short and Fun

I end with a short, fun participation piece. "A Penny and a Half" works well here. In this Chilean folktale, the main character keeps buying more and more animals until he finally buys a guitar and all of the animals dance. Simple. I bring up participants to act the role of the various animals. I just keep adding animals to the tale until the entire class is onstage. This enables everyone to get up and dance and move. The story can be stretched or contracted to fit the time allowed. I can add more animals to stretch or add seven ducks at a time to shorten the tale. A story with slots that can be filled with repeated characters allows you to end right on time and look like you planned things out exactly!

## Future Contact

Be sure to put your contact information on your handouts, and remind the participants that you are available for future questions and help they may need.

*Chapter 11*

# Translation into a Signed Language

*In this chapter Lois Sprengnether Keel, a storyteller who uses sign language with her hearing impaired daughter, and Karee Wardrop, a professional sign interpreter, speak of using ASL to translate stories.*

## TELLING WITH SIGN LANGUAGE TRANSLATION
### by Lois Sprengnether Keel

*Lois Sprengnether Keel discusses several issues that arise when a teller is translated into sign.*

### Sign Languages

American Sign Language (ASL) used to be the fourth most utilized language in the United States, but it has moved to the third most used and is becoming well established in that position for more reasons than just its usage by the deaf. When a child experiences a language delay for whatever reason, ASL is often taught. It also can work with special needs audiences of many kinds.

Advocates of "baby sign" advise young parents to talk and simultaneously sign to infants as soon as a child begins to point. Children learn language quicker and communicate better and earlier when both forms of language are used. Researchers even claim it raises IQ levels by 12 points. This reflects a major change in thinking from days when parents were told signing delayed speech. In addition, more people are learning American Sign Language because of its acceptance by many colleges and universities for credit as a "foreign language."

Sign language's visibility has increased because of several factors. Churches are eager to reach all potential members, including those with a hearing impairment. *Sesame Street* characters show the ease of learning ASL and its usefulness to both children and their parents. The Americans with Disabilities Act requires sign language assistance where needed, leading many event organizers to include ASL interpreters. People often comment on the beauty of signing after seeing it at church or other events, especially when accompanying song lyrics.

As a storyteller it helps to learn more about signing. There will be times when an interpreter will translate what you say. If you know ASL you also may wish to be able to tell stories in both voice and sign.

Signing was introduced into the United States from France. As a result, ASL tends to use French word order, which can confuse a storyteller when looking at an interpreter. In addition, there is the same sort of time lag common when any language is interpreted.

So far, ASL has been presumed to be the standard needed when signing occurs, but communication by use of signs in actual practice is less rigid. It runs in a spectrum from straight mime—which may be necessary to describe some actions—through ASL and continues on to Signed English. Signed English was created to help deaf children learn English grammar and parts of speech. It includes filler words such as *the* and other words that are implied but omitted in ASL, and even adds word endings such as *ing*. In ASL the same sign can represent more than one form of a word; for example, one sign can mean both *usually* and *use*. Signed English tends to move at a slower pace because its purpose is instructional and more detailed than typical sign language communication. Also on that spectrum of communication is Pidgin Sign, which adapts signing to an English word order. This tends to be used especially when the speaker is telling simultaneously in voice and sign. Because the goal is communication, members of your audience may differ as to where they are on this spectrum of communication.

Some are pure ASL, especially as it has become widely used as the standard for interpreter certification. Possibly such individuals may not even want initialized signs. Initialized signs are where the sign begins with its first letter finger spelled as part of the sign. Some may be accustomed to Pidgin Sign as they communicate a great deal with hearing people who talk and sign simultaneously. The sign for *hearing* is a perfect example of this, as it has nothing to do with the ear or listening; rather it uses the sign for *talking* because those who hear also usually talk. Children in school may still be learning Signed English, and aspects of it may be used to convey an academic or formal style of communicating.

### Finger Spelling and the Creation of Name Signs

Another aspect of communicating includes finger spelling. Names, as well as words for which an interpreter does not know an appropriate sign, require spelling out the word using the letters of the Manual Alphabet. This can be tricky when a story uses many proper names or foreign words. Deaf audience members usually follow and guess what a finger-spelled word is going to be, but it is tiring for both the interpreter and the person watching the interpreter. Just as hearing people use nicknames, the deaf may use name signs as a short way to say a person's name. The name sign generally uses the initial letter of a name and often is placed on the body in a place that matches that person's most distinctive feature. Interpreters often place their initial letter in the crook of the elbow as interpreters move their forearms so much when signing.

Creating a name sign can be tricky and should always be checked with deaf adults. An interpreter once decided she was tired of being name signed inside her elbow. She decided that her smile was her best feature and decided to place her initial letter, which was *L*, at her mouth and take it upward in a smile. The deaf adults for whom she interpreted let her know this was the sign for *leopard*, because it was an initialized form of the sign for *cat*. The interpreter had skin spotted from years of acne and quickly changed back to placing her *L* inside her elbow. Additionally, a sign may already be in use for another individual. Another person whose name began with *L* decided to use the sign for *lucky*. Her older aunt scolded her, saying that she had been using that name sign long before her niece. The aunt promptly assigned the niece the name sign of *lazy*. Yet another individual whose name began with *A* had striking blond hair and wanted to place an *A* on it, but was warned that he was using a vulgar word. A man with a mustache whose name begins with *H* shouldn't use that for his name sign, as it is the name sign for *Hitler*, and many will automatically think of this well-known person when it is used. Other common name signs exist. Unlike other languages, there is no way of seeing a sign and looking it up for the reverse into English. For all of these reasons, before an interpreter chooses a name sign for himself or herself or during a story, it should be checked with deaf adults to be sure it is acceptable.

### Working with the Interpreter

Certified interpreters are used to finger spelling and catching names without advance notice, but providing them with video or audio recordings, printed copies of stories, a summary of a story, or at least a list of names or unusual words in a story to be told can help produce a better result. This is especially true for music, poetry, and foreign words. If the music has no lyrics, an interpreter signs *music*, often in time to the beat, to explain the lull in interpreting. Similarly, if a string of foreign conversation is used and the audience is not expected to know what is said, the interpreter signs that this is what is happening.

In some instances an interpreter may explain what is occurring if the audience appears puzzled. Similarly, finger spelling or initializing words does not work when signing is done for children too young to understand it. In such instances the signs must convey the concept; otherwise miming may be used. Especially if an interpreter needs to be sure the audience sees what the storyteller is doing, one of two things may be done: the interpreter may point to the storyteller in an invitation to watch without a split in focus—best when words or signs are not necessary—or the interpreter may be placed close to the storyteller, shadowing the storyteller.

Awareness of an interpreter can be distracting, but the storyteller should try to ignore what can probably be seen on the edge of his or her vision. It is important also to place the interpreter in good light for being seen and near the deaf to view. Sometimes when a storyteller has said something difficult for an interpreter to sign, such as a string of names or nonsense words, a storyteller may pause to allow the interpreter to catch up. It even can be a form of play between the storyteller and the interpreter when the situation of the telling and the personalities of the two permit it.

If the storyteller uses Native American sign language, there are both differences and similarities in signs, just as signing has differences between countries.

An example of the variation in sign language of countries occurs when *turtle* is signed in the United States by the thumb peeking in and out from under the fist of the other hand. The Canadian sign for *turtle* conveys the concept of swimming, as one outstretched hand is placed on top of the other with palms down, while the thumbs circle in a swimming motion. Additionally, regional or local differences can occur with signs. *Picnic* is a commonly noted example of a word or concept with many different signs. Even the song, "Let's Call the Whole Thing Off," which mentions *tomato* with either a long "A" or the "Ah" sound, is reflected in signing, as more than one form of sign exists for *tomato*. Ethnic groups and nations have also received some new signs in an attempt at political correctness, but the choice of sign depends on which sign is known and used by the audience. Additionally, differences can exist by age, with children using something an older adult might not consider proper, such as the difference between the sign for *restroom* and *toilet* or the sign for *children* versus *kids*. The choices of signs are usually not of great concern to a storyteller if an interpreter is provided and the storyteller pays no attention to the interpreting.

Not every situation uses a certified interpreter. Churches often use people signing without certification. Libraries and recreation departments may also utilize non-certified signers or sign language students in an attempt to keep expenses down. The signer gets little pay but maintains and improves sign language skills. Planning programs in these situations calls for advance preparation between the signer and the storyteller. Certain times it may be difficult to obtain someone to sign, such as a Wednesday evening, when church services may require the signer.

Additional choices of signs are of interest if the storyteller knows sign language and attempts to tell in voice and sign language simultaneously. In such situations the signing tends more toward Pidgin Sign sequence rather than ASL, as most expressions follow the words told. In such circumstances the pace of telling may be slowed by the signing. Word choice may change to fit signs the storyteller knows or wishes to use. When this is the case, it is worthwhile to practice such stories with deaf individuals and also with interpreters. When words must be finger spelled, unless the word is very short, it can be done by voicing each letter as it is finger spelled and then the word said. Another way to tell would be to sign first and then say what was signed, but this is the slowest way to tell and many stories will not accommodate it.

Interpreters are familiar with the need to dress for ease of visibility, but a storyteller signing may need to remember that clothing should be in contrast to skin tones and without distracting patterns. A light-skinned teller who is signing should wear a dark top, whereas a dark-skinned teller would wear a light-colored top.

### Voice Interpreters for Deaf Storytellers

Finally, not all interpreting is from voice to sign. Deaf storytellers require an oral interpreter of their signs when telling to a hearing audience. Once again, it may help to provide a written account. In this case what is written would either be by the deaf storyteller, or it may be a written form of what is understood by the oral interpreter. This is necessary because, unlike other languages, a dictionary of signs does not exist to provide a means of looking up from sign to word—only word to sign. The way to verify what a sign means is by repeating the sign and then asking its meaning. In contrast, a sign can always be finger spelled and then repeated to teach what a sign means.

### Providing a Sign Interpreter

Often interpreters are provided at events and yet no deaf audience members appear. This does not mean it was unnecessary. Publicity to create an audience is crucial and it can take time to build such an audience. People requiring sign language interpreting deserve the same right to decide whether to attend with little or no advance notice as do other audience members. In addition we all are "TABs—Temporarily Able Bodied," and so it helps to have audience awareness of what is often a hidden disability. Signing at events, as noted in the introduction to this article, also has increased interest in young people choosing to become interpreters or at least in many people of all ages learning to sign.

## HOW DO YOU SIGN *SCALLYWAG?*
## AN INTERPRETER AT WORK

by Karee Wardrop

*Here is the other side of the coin. A professional interpreter writes of working with tellers and offers us some advice.*

How do you sign *scallywag?* This is undoubtedly the most often asked question of interpreters. "How do you sign . . . " and inevitably the word in question is something colorful that has no one-sign equivalent. Or the question is asked about a particularly memorable sign that was used, and there is no one-word English equivalent. The more I interpret, the more I believe that true one-to-one lexical item equivalents between languages are rare. In order to understand why this is true, it may help to understand some basics not only about the linguistics involved but also about the actual process of interpreting.

American Sign Language (ASL) interpreters live in a world of immediacy. We work in face-to-face communication most of the time. We are face to face in the doctor's office, in the board room, at the family gathering, at the convention planning meeting—face to face anywhere a deaf party and a hearing party want to communicate with each other but do not understand or use each other's languages well enough to communicate accurately and thoroughly. What we as interpreters do, briefly, is this: we assess the meaning and spirit of a communication in one language/culture and accurately and thoroughly deliver the equivalent meaning and spirit in the second language/culture without deletions or additions—in regards to either information or personal opinion. Our goal is not only accuracy but also invisibility really. Because we want the people who came to communicate with each other to be able to do so, we are as unobtrusive as possible, making the communication as direct as possible.

We deliver the message, and the spirit of the message, completely and accurately. This means we consider not only the language being used—the vocabulary, the grammar, the phrasing, the colloquialisms—but also the spirit of the deliverer: the prosodic elements, the mood, the intent . . . the ambiguities when ambiguous, the threats when threatening, the sarcasm, and such. We also take into consideration the person who is communicating—how would the counterpart in the target language speak? A middle-aged businesswoman from Seattle, for example, makes different language choices than a middle school boy from Richmond. In some respects, experienced interpreters are natural working partners with storytellers. We, as experienced certified interpreters, find ourselves in such a variety of situations with so many different kinds of people that our understanding of character and voice is admirable; our lexicons are likewise rich.

When we are asked to interpret a storytelling, we consider it a luxurious task. This is when we become translators for a time. Stories are often provided in some fixed form—either written English or signed ASL. Even when not written down, a storyteller can usually at least outline, if not recite completely, the story to be told. When this is true, the translator takes time to examine the fixed form—analyze the language being used, the voice of the characters, the moral, the intent, the overall dramatic arc of the piece, the subtle or hidden meanings. All of this information is used to create an equivalent story in the target language/culture. We ask ourselves, what is this story trying to say? How is it saying it? What language is being used, in what tone, and with which literary devices?

When the performance time arrives, the translator takes all of her work and uses it as a foundation, but retransforms into interpreter, to be ready to work spontaneously in the immediate moment, between a storyteller and a particular audience. In order to provide as accurate an interpretation as possible, the translator asks the teller: Why this story? What are you trying to get across to this particular audience? If there is one thing you want them to remember what would it be? Is this a history lesson, a moral lesson, an exercise in silliness? All of these answers will inform the interpreter's choices as she interprets. She must be ready to adjust vocabulary choices, phrasings. On occasion, when a particular audience revels in an unforeseen aspect of the story and the teller is adroit in adjusting on his feet, sometimes even the moral gets shifted. The point is that you, the teller, have control. It is your story, and our job as the interpreter is to deliver your story as you tell it in the moment. Translation helps prepare us, but in the moment we are interpreting.

So what about *scallywag*? How do you sign it? If you ask ten different deaf native ASL signers this question—which, by the way, is whom you should ask when looking for signs—you may see ten different answers. As I said earlier, the longer I interpret the more I believe that one-to-one equivalencies between languages are hard to come by. Yes, you can learn the word for *table* or *book* or other concrete concepts in as many languages as you like. That initial equivalence quickly gives way, however, to the many other definitions and connotations that any given word/sign has. Think for just a minute about those two everyday words, *table* and *book*. Now check your favorite dictionary to see how many definitions each word has.

Although there are surface-level equivalences between languages, it is the secondary meanings, the meanings that give a lexical item color and texture in a culture, and grit or glory in a story, may be very different in a second language. Why does a storyteller choose one word over another? For precisely those reasons—the word has a definite meaning, secondary subtle meanings, and, I'd venture to say, a personal meaning as well.

Sometimes English words' *meanings* don't matter much at all, because the words are chosen for their auditory qualities . . . *hissing, chomping, grunting, slapping,* whispered words, alliterative words, stormy words. These, of course, have no *direct* equivalent in a visual language, but the auditory components can translate into visual components that bring the same understanding and emotional effect to those for whom the visual language is their first language.

The first level a speaker works with is single words. Each word lives within a phrase, and each phrase lives within a context, a setting; it is easy to see how word-for-word "translations" are useless. Compound this with a particular character who is speaking. Perhaps the character, who is normally a smooth talker (a trait that already comes with its own specialized lexicon), is currently anxious for some reason. Is anxiety conveyed the same way in different cultures? Is anticipation? What about something like conscious ambiguity?

ASL is a visual language. Not only do one-to-one equivalencies rarely exist between it and English, but in trying to find them we are comparing apples to rocket science. One language depends on vocal production of linear grammatical information that is received auditorily; the other language relies on use of physical space, postural and facial grammar, as well as speed, direction, and intensity of movement to convey grammatical and prosodic information. Both are full languages with grammatical rules, gigantic lexicons, and rich cultural histories.

How do you sign *scallywag*? You can see that it depends on why it is used in the story, who uses the word, and what is the intention behind the word. Is it repeated? Is it a catchword to carry the story? And so on. Sometimes there may be an equivalent in the second language. At other times the word in question does not have an outright word-for-word equivalent, but its *presence* is present. It may be embedded elsewhere in the phrase, or it may be conveyed, for example, through the other adverbs chosen for that character in the second language that will make the *scallywagness* obvious.

Different languages/cultures have different ways of expressing themselves. Remember that the job of the interpreter is to convey the teller's story accurately into the target language/culture. We want the target audience to have as close to the same experience as the audience that is receiving the story in the teller's language. Words may not be exactly the same, but meaning, intent, and spirit will be. Because different languages have different modes, there are some functional differences as well. Because of grammar structural differences, timing may vary so that, consequently, laughs may come at slightly different times, or the "aha!" moment may be slightly delayed or even premature. Rest assured, though, that all of your story is there in all its glory.

For storytellers who are considering using ASL within spoken English storytelling, please be careful. Signs are accessible to us as hearing people because we can speak our words and move our hands in what looks like language at the same time. We cannot speak English and Spanish at the same time, so we don't try. The same holds true for English and ASL—we cannot speak English and sign ASL at the same time either. The two languages are grammatically so disparate that it is not possible to do and make any sense in either language. It just *appears* that it is possible—to those who are not bilingual.

Please also remember that you are borrowing from a language with a rich heritage and a culture of people who cherish their language. Learning some signs from a book doesn't guarantee that you are using the "right" sign for your story. Gestures—those physical actions that we all understand no matter what culture we are from, the shoulder shrug, the head nod, the pointing finger—are all wonderful in storytelling for so many reasons. Signs are not gestures and they are not words. Signs are part of a language used proudly by millions.

How do you sign *scallywag*? The answer, of course, is, it all depends.

*Chapter 12*

# Cultural Considerations

In this chapter tellers consider the effects of culture on translation. Michael Harvey writes of what he calls British, French, and Welsh "cultural games." Cathy Spagnoli discusses her work in Asian cultures. David Titus reveals cultural mishaps while telling in Nepal, Estonia, and Mongolia. And Mama Edie Armstrong tells of sharing tales with Cantonese-speaking children and in other multicultural settings.

## HOW CULTURES AFFECT THE TELLINGS
### by Michael Harvey

*Through an email exchange, Michael Harvey expressed some interesting thoughts about the cultural games storytellers and audiences play.*

### Differing Cultural Games

Michael Harvey, who tells mostly in English, speaks

I also tell in French and I have noticed that the three languages not only have a different music but also a set of social games that can be employed to make the telling of the same story in different languages a significantly different cultural event.

I ask Michael to elaborate on what he means

There seem to be different cultural games available in each language.

## British Audiences

We Brits are not meant to "show-off." It's very bad form and definitely not cricket. Also direct reference to anything remotely problematic may cause embarrassment, which is a kind of social death. This means we have developed a kind of code whereby we can say one thing and mean another. This infuriates everyone else, especially those from a Latin culture. "Why can't you just say what you mean?" The upside of this is that we can do irony in our performing (but not in a showy way, of course!). We have gotten so used to reading between the lines that we have become quite fluent in that liminal space—very handy in a story, which is another kind of liminal space. This means that, particularly for adult audiences, we can play in the gaps between the story and the event, between the two worlds that are in contact during the telling, and between what I say and what I describe happening. There is a gap between my description of an action and what "actually" happened, which the audience can imaginatively fill in.

Performers here frequently underplay their own status in order to gain rapport with the audience and then grab the story and go for it once everyone knows it's "OK." Once this kind of reaction is understood, it can be fun and useful to play against it. We feel safe around endearing vagueness (think of some of the characters played by Hugh Grant), and it keeps everyone awake to puncture that with something more direct and punchy.

I've just reread the above and can immediately think of many exceptions to the rule. It would be safest to read what I've written as a very subjective account applying mainly to me!

## Welsh Audiences

Most of the work I do is in schools in Wales, and to be honest I don't see a great difference between English medium and Welsh medium schools. However, in an evening performance in primarily Welsh-speaking areas (North and West), the difference is marked. First of all, you need to know that I am not Welsh. I was born in Glasgow, arrived over twenty years ago, and after a few years began learning the language out of idle curiosity and one thing led to another.

Everyone knows everyone else here, so a separation of audience and performer is never really possible. You can never have the anonymity of a stage persona because everyone knows who you "really" are. The first conversation that two people from Welsh-speaking areas who do not know each other have will be about how they are connected by mutual acquaintances. Then a relationship can be developed—but until you know to "whom" you're talking, that is not possible. The predominant social dynamic is "belonging."

This means that I cannot walk onto stage as the "professional storyteller." I have to be socially licensed. This usually means some kind of acceptance by being promoted by the right person/body. It means I'm "in." Many people move to Wales (nice scenery, cheaper houses) and either live their lives separately or feel rebuffed because they don't get this dynamic.

When I am in front of one of those audiences, I do not feel that I am there to impress them but to remind them of stories they already know. This means the reactions can be muted, which was difficult at first because I wasn't getting the applause strokes I was used to, but they listen in a totally different way. They laugh less, have a "thirst" for the story (that's what it feels like from where I'm standing), and dive into the darker moments of the story in ways that I have not encountered elsewhere. The material I've been telling in these contexts has been mainly stuff from the Mabinogi, and the subtext to the event is often one of linguistic and cultural survival against the odds. Their reaction to the description of the battle in Ireland in the story of Branwen where almost everyone is killed, for example, felt profoundly deeper and darker than that of other audiences. At the end of the story they sat in this darkness for a long time, and I felt that they "knew" it culturally.

## French Audiences

I find telling in French for Francophone audiences really liberating (as long as I am on top of the language). There you are expected to take the stage with assurance and *élan*, and any Anglo-apologetic style of presentation is just not possible. Culture is something to be celebrated and enjoyed rather than justified as in the United Kingdom, and my feeling is that people are very much with you as you tell. *L'amour* is also totally different to *love* in stories. There is nothing coy or soppy about it, and no one in the audience will make that "awww" noise when the couple finally does get together.

The French do have a love of hierarchy and order, which I know has restricted some people's opportunities in France; however, I try to sidestep this by gleefully embracing the role of foreign idiot!

---

## TELLING IN OTHER LANGUAGES: PROBLEMS AND SOLUTIONS
by Cathy Spagnoli

*Cathy Spagnoli spends at least half of her year in Asia, either at her second home in South India or on tour in Japan, Singapore, Korea, and elsewhere. So, much of her work is done via translation. She shares here some of the issues she encounters in her work.*

### Images

Although I can get by in several Asian languages, I'm not fluent in any of them, so I try to research images to use from the language, along with greetings, formulas, and so on. I keep lists of images that I've heard storytellers use or that I have read in storytelling notes from that culture: "lightning like a knife of fire, or as pretty as a dragon's daughter" (Hmong); "as lonely as a single wild goose, or as light as the wing of a dragonfly" (Korean).

Sometimes, the image is very important in the culture and so I need to use it, instead of a Western equivalent. I discovered in telling the Khmer epic, *Tum Teav*, that an offering of love in Cambodia would not be a rose, but rather a betel nut (to chew). For the picture book, *Judge Rabbit and the Tree Spirit*, I worked with a group of Cambodian women who pieced the story together in Khmer, and then Lina Mao Wall and I worked on a translation. In one part, I wrote that a man walked sadly away or something just as boring. Then Lina, fortunately, mentioned that in the Khmer language, one would say sadness followed him like a shadow. I changed the words right away!

### Nuance and Definition

Recently, when a translator was translating one of my Judge Rabbit stories into Korean, he asked why I had used the word *judge* in Judge Rabbit. He said that a Korean would never place it in front of an animal's name, even if the animal were wise, for *judge* referred only to humans and was purely a legal term. I told him how important the character of Judge Rabbit is to Cambodians, and finally he decided to use an older Korean word for the wise man in the village who would solve problems centuries ago.

In Japan, I love to tell the story "I'm Coming," in which body parts of a ghost fall down the chimney. But we always have to explain beforehand that a ghost in the United States can have hands and legs, because the Japanese *yure* has no legs; it simply floats and thus doesn't fit so well in this tale!

### Onomatopeia

English is not known for its rich range of sound words, but so many other languages have a great store. I try to collect different sound words in Asian languages so that I can use them at times while telling to liven up a tale. It's always sad to me when a translator drops these treasures or converts them to some weaker English variant.

However, such sound words, placed in an English tale for English listeners, lose meaning, too. They add an interesting sound and wake up our listeners' ears, but of course, they can't convey the nuances and the shades of meaning/feeling that they do to the native speaker/listener.

## Formality

English is a very egalitarian language and that presents problems, too, in translation. A language such as Korean, with its many different types of courteous language and degrees of politeness, loses much when it's translated into English in which there is only one *you* for high and low, and little alternative vocabulary to differentiate levels in society.

When we were adding the Khmer translation to the pictures of Judge Rabbit, we used several lines for each page/drawing—a type of summary rather than a word-for-word or line-by-line translation. I had no way of knowing how the translation sounded, but I trusted my coworker and she did a fine job. However, she did a fine job in a formal way, for that was her background. When I had some people in early childhood and primary schools read the book—after it had been published—they pointed out that it was in very formal Khmer language, not the type that would be used to tell a story to young children!

Likewise, in India years ago we produced various brochures and booklets for use in schools. One, for day care providers, called *Priya Pudikindren* ("Priya Learns"), shared low-cost teaching ideas. But we had to go through three different translations to get the right tone. The first was by a writer friend, but his translation was much too elegant for a day care provider. The second was from a high school teacher—not so lovely, but still too difficult. Finally, my husband and a friend worked together and used much simpler, livelier language to finally get the job done the right way for those young readers!

## Gesture

When telling in another country, translating gestures becomes very important. Some offensive gestures need to be avoided—touching someone on the head in some cultures, or the way one beckons with a hand in others. Other gestures can confuse: several years ago, I happily signed "London Bridge" to many audiences across Japan. My best friend watched my last program and then said softly afterward, "Cathy, I hate to tell you but the sign for a lady you used is just like our sign for *yakuza*–gangster." So all across Japan, I had happily signed "my fair *yakuza*" to end "London Bridge" with an unusual twist!

Another time, when I was telling *Kaza Jizo*, about the kind man who gives his hats to the *Jizo* statues, I had the man trying to sell his hats rather desperately at the end of the day, with broad gestures and a loud voice. Two years later, when I was back in Japan, another friend kindly asked me to change the way I told the tale. She said that I sold the hats with too big a way, like Ōsaka style! But the story came from the north of Japan and there, they would sell with a much quieter voice and style.

## Illustration

Accuracy in illustration is an important consideration in translated works. When checking proof sheets for *Judge Rabbit Helps the Fish*, I was very upset to find a crayfish drawn instead of the *kr'an* fish, a fish important to the culture and the story. Luckily, after an involved search, we did locate one and now the book has the correct fish!

## Translation in Performance

Working across cultures in performance creates all kinds of interesting challenges. In Bangladesh, while telling a story with two Bangla musicians, I felt the music should be fast and rather furious at a certain point, to underline the story's mood. Yet they played a slow raga melody. I tried with my hands to suggest a faster pace, but they continued in the same way. At the end of the rehearsal, they told me very clearly that the audience would understand exactly the right mood, from that raga, and not from any of my ideas! They were right . . . . In Japan, I'm often thrown by the use of *ma* ("space/pause"). When I think it's time to move on with some music or some words, the Japanese artists often have a very different sense of timing.

Bilingual telling is also a learning experience. When I tell with Japanese teller Kazu Honda, we sometimes plays with variations in timing and the other riches of tandem telling. Other times, we tell the same (short) story all the way through in both languages—to show the flow of the language and the difference in feeling.

When I tell alone to those with limited English, I often need some interpretation. But I've had some disastrous results with well-meaning but ill-prepared interpreters, whether they were telling just an outline first or actually trying to break into (and up) the story. Now I find it best either to have someone I trust give a small summary before each story or to provide a simple translation in the program. In Japan, such programs are often very lovely, of fine paper, and obviously something to keep fondly (and one hopes, to reread and thus to re-create the storytelling).

---

## TRANSLATING MISHAPS
### by David Titus

*Traveling string-figure missionary and storyteller David Titus sends notes about his many amusing, and maybe not so amusing, mishaps with translators.*

### Tales That Don't Work via Sign Language Interpretation

I have had a couple of interesting things happen when I had interpreters for the hearing-impaired members of the audience. In one instance I was starting to tell "Master of All Masters," the English tale with nonsense words in it that you say again all at once at the end. The interpreter knew the story and when I started the story, she just threw up her hands and sat down, knowing that she could not do justice to it. Another time, I was telling a humorous hunting story, "The Skoon Kin Hunting," that had a lot of wordplay in it . . . *dear dog* and *deer dog*, *cents* and *scents*, and similar things. The story was a complete flop with that audience because those things must be heard.

### Language Translators Who "Take Over" the Story

I tell stories using string figures and then teach some of the figures to the audience. In two specific instances in Latvia, I had told the story and was then teaching one of the figures. Both of these times the interpreters had been with me and translated the story three or four times . . . they were familiar with it. I was in the midst of teaching the figure and was not going fast enough for the translators. In each instance the translator stepped in front of me and taught the figure perfectly . . . just ahead of me. I stopped talking and decided that I could not use them for translators anymore, but did have two disciples now.

Another time, in Nepal, I was trying to explain how to do the string figure and was saying things such as "under" or "go over," and "bring the string through with the thumb" or "with the little finger." The translator stood there and made each move and said in the native language . . . "like so," "like so," and "like so" to the moves that I made.

In Mongolia I had hired a translator for the month. He traveled with me and was very capable in all instances except when he knew the answer. If someone would ask a question that he knew the answer to, he would respond and not bother to translate. When called on this, he said, "But I knew the answer." He never understood the idea that his job was to translate everything.

## Alternating Languages Line by Line

I had a lot of fun with the story "Nothing Has Been Going On Since You've Been Gone." I was working with a group of high school students in Eastern Europe. My translator, a very outgoing person, picked up the idea of storytelling very fast. We worked it out ahead of time to have him tell part of the story in Estonian, and I would say part in English. I taught him the story and he was very good at understanding it and ready to have fun. It went like this: first, the introduction in which I talked and he translated; then we launched into the story.

English:    What's been going on since I've been gone?
Estonian:   Nothing.
English:    Nothing?
Estonian:   No, not a thing, except your dog died.
English:    My dog died. How did he die?
Estonian:   Don't know. Might be that he ate the burned horse flesh and died.
English:    Burned horse flesh? Where did he get burned horse flesh?
Estonian:   "Well, it might have been from your barn. When your barn burned down, it burned the horses and the dog ate the burned horse flesh and died.
English:    How did my barn burn down?

The high school kids knew just enough English to realize that I was responding to what he was saying and thought that I understood everything that he was saying in Estonian. They were amazed at my language abilities in such a short time. We really had them going.

## *Goff, Goff! Wowser, Wowser!* Getting the Animal Sounds Right

I have found that in stories that have the sound of an animal, it is very important to have the animal make the sound that it would in that country.

People are listening to the English and become confused when the animals make different noises. Dogs in Russia say, "Goff, goff," whereas in other places they say, "Wowser, wowser" or "Wow, wow." In the story of "Why It's Important to Be Bilingual," in which the mouse is walking along and meets a cat, then barks at it and it runs away, I tell an embellished form of the story with the translator translating. I have done my homework and find out what a mouse, cat, and dog sound like in that country. I have talked with the translator and explained when to stop translating. We then tell the story and when I get to the part where the mouse barks and the cat runs away, the translator does not translate that. By then the audience knows what just happened and then we come back with the moral.

## Working with the Translator

I talk to the translator ahead of time to tell the gist of the story. If there are any unfamiliar words or names, I explain them. I also try to listen to the translator to see whether I think he is telling all of the story. Sometimes the translator changes things, and you can tell from words that sound similar what has happened. I have even had translators change the focus of the talk. Usually someone in the audience who knows both languages will say, "Boy, your story was about 'Grace' and it sure came out to be a story of 'Works.'"

## Watch Those Gestures!

Another problem that I have had to work through is the question of gesture. In South Africa, using the index and middle finger to signify the number 2 is a very rude gesture, much as "flipping a bird." Also in England, I have to use the thumb and index finger. Standing with my hands in my pockets is rude in Lithuania. Using a handkerchief in front of American kids may bring a giggle, but in Mongolia it completely floors them. They don't have such things. In one of the string figures, I have people hold the string in their fist then stick out the index and point . . . I heard one translator saying "pistola" in giving the directions. That works there, but it was not what I said.

## How Long Does It Take to Say the Lord's Prayer?

One trap can be to think translators are adding to or not telling all simply because they are taking such a long time or not taking much time. That can be just how the language is. In Estonia, the "Lord's Prayer" in Estonian and English can start at the same time and end at almost exactly the same time if two people are saying it simultaneously. On the other hand, in one country to the South, Latvia, when I am completely done with it, the translator is only halfway through. It takes almost twice as much time to say something in Latvian.

Some things just don't translate. People in the Kalahari Desert or the Mongolian Steppes or the foothills of the Himalayas just don't have the same perspective as do people in the suburbs of Houston. On the other hand, people in small Alaskan villages understand some of the basic lives of folktale characters better than the inner-city kids from Chicago do.

---

## THE ROAD TO REACHING A MULTILINGUAL AUDIENCE
### by Mama Edie Armstrong

*Mama Edie Armstrong, storyteller and speech pathologist, blends Spanish and other languages into her stories to help the tales reach her multilingual audiences. Drawing on her experience telling to children from Cantonese-speaking homes and also telling in many multicultural settings, she lays out some basic steps to consider in multicultural storytelling.*

### Sharing Tales with Young Children from Cantonese-Speaking Homes

After giving a workshop at the Harold Washington Library for teachers on the power of including storytelling in the regular academic curriculum, I received a call from a young teacher named Theresa from the Chinese-American Service League in Chicago. She asked if I would come and provide a performance for the children in their after-school program. They ranged in age from five to about twelve years old. I asked Theresa whether the children spoke English, as my Cantonese was a little rusty. She laughed and said that the little ones would probably have the greatest challenge, as most of them were from homes where Cantonese was the primary—and often the only—language spoken. But she assured me that the older children who were learning English would very likely understand more than they would be able to actually say themselves. Of course, this is the typical pattern, where despite one's age, language, or culture, comprehension generally precedes expression. It is similar to a baby understanding "No, no!" or "More cookie?" or "Bring that to me," before the child can actually say any part of these expressions. Theresa also reflected that, from the presentation I provided to the teachers at the library, she had faith that the amount of facial and other bodily expressions that I provided would likely contribute well to their understanding. So, I told her that if she was willing to try, then so was I.

Although most of my stories are from the African Diaspora (African-rooted cultures of the world, i.e., those present in Africa, the Caribbean, the Americas, etc.), I chose for this day also to tell at least one Chinese story in order to honor the culture of the children who were my audience.

The event was wonderful. I was warmly received by everyone, although at first, the children were slow to respond openly. Cultural norms, no doubt, played a role, as many traditional Chinese children often seem less freely expressive in a structured setting in the presence of adults than many American children whose English-speaking families have lived in this country for many generations.

Other contributors to this reticent response pattern most likely included lack of familiarity with me, my African attire, and my head wrap, not knowing what they might expect from me, and not knowing what my expectations were of them. But in an appreciably short space of time, the initial tension and reluctance melted away and ushered in a joyful spirit instead.

Many of the children did seem to understand the majority of the basic concepts that I was relating. This was evidenced by their laughter in appropriate places, their expected looks of surprise, and even their looks of disapproval of a character's actions, such as the cat stealing all the meat away from the dog after they had both helped to pay for it! This was the principal conflict in the story of "Why Dogs Chase Cats." I also observed the children's facial expressions of sympathy and compassion, which further reflected their emotional involvement in the story. Their willingness to try to answer questions, to repeat the presented words and phrases in English or even the African languages, and/or to sing along was also evidence of their openness and receptivity to the experience. Everyone seemed to have had a great time. The teachers were happy and so was I.

### Mama Edie's List of Multilingual Storytelling Considerations

Thinking through my approach to this performance, I developed "Mama Edie's List of Multilingual Storytelling Considerations" (MELOMSC) in order to best facilitate comprehension and enjoyment.

### Cultural Background Information

1. Learn from the inviting hosts what the cultural blend of the audience is likely to be.

2. Come to the performance prepared with at least some functional information about the various cultures likely to be present. When possible, speak with individuals from some of those cultures before the presentation to learn from them. The information you research may not be presented during the performance, but it will provide background and sensitivity for your telling. It gave me great pleasure, for example, while telling to ten- to twelve-year-old children from many cultures at an ESL (English as a Second Language) school in Rochester, New York, to know a little Amharic, spoken by the Ethiopian children there. This was a performance done on behalf of the National Association of Black Storytellers. After a couple of my stories, the children shared some of their own personal stories of life in their countries. Some had come from Bosnia, Sudan, Somalia, and other countries at war. But then, much to their surprise and delight, I engaged them all in a Tegrinia dance, done with the shoulders by Ethiopians, Eritreans, and Somalians. Their eyes became large and their smiles wide as they watched me dance. They laughed and clapped and danced with me to their own music that the teacher had taped for them. One of the Ethiopian boys sang and the party was on! We were connected, and that's what storytelling is about.

3. Tell stories from at least two of the several cultures likely to be present. They can be short but can contribute well to a sense of bonding. Create gracious transitions that would address the potential and yet unspoken question, "Why not a story from *my* people?" Remember that everyone wants to be acknowledged, especially when living in a country—and not by choice—that is away from "home."

4. Be sensitive to the fact that different people have varying response patterns. For example, many people of African descent—no matter where in the world they have been born or raised—flow quite naturally into call-and-response patterns. This is a very African interactional style, whether in public presentations in a theater, on the playground, or in church. African audience members may therefore offer appropriately spontaneous contributions to storytelling performances. These can initially be a little disorienting to a storyteller unfamiliar with this custom. In time, however, the teller comes to understand that it is simply a reflection of the appreciation and connection that she has facilitated.

5. Become acquainted with some of the holidays of various audience members and the concepts behind them. Acquire some appreciation for the level of importance that these holidays may currently have to that community. This may serve a teller and audience particularly well considering the time of year of one's presentation.

## Specific Linguistic Considerations

1. Find out the average level of English proficiency that the audience is likely to have. This will help in planning how much one can rely on English only and also the number of and degree to which other techniques may need to be employed.
2. Keep the language concepts simple.
3. Keep the sentences short.
4. Be extra sensitive to making effective eye contact with *every*one.
5. The teller's eyes and other facial expressions should relay all the emotion that one cannot say in the audience's own language.
6. Use various positions in space to hold the audience's attention and to relay the action of the story.
7. Repeat what was just said in a different and/or particularly engaging way if their expressions reflect that they didn't get it the first time. Employ other physical movements or expressions to assist if needed.
8. Use character voices and variations in pitch, volume, timing, and tone to better hold their attention and to relate the mood or intent of an expression that cannot be verbally expressed.
9. Carefully monitor the rate of speech and articulate clarity without overexaggerating beyond comprehension.
10. Ask simple questions from time to time to monitor the audience understanding and to make necessary adjustments.
11. Make use of the call-and-response components of the story to engage the listeners in the telling process. This will also facilitate their learning of the English language.
12. Employ music and melodic phrases or chants to keep those most challenged with comprehension at least feeling as though they are a part of the journey.
13. Pay careful attention to *everything*.
14. Be grateful for and encouraged by elicited responses.
15. Where language fails . . . sing!
16. Audience members should know that the teller is happy to be there.
17. Determine that this is going to be a fun experience for all!

## Using Unfamiliar Languages:
## Blending Speech Pathology and Storytelling

Providing services as a speech and language pathologist, storyteller, and musician has been a naturally evolving and wonderfully rewarding blending of professions for me. I have always been fascinated by the power, origins, and meanings of words and other sounds as well. These sounds include vocal and other instrumental music, the melody in the linguistic expressions of various languages, wind chimes, sounds of the wind itself, bird calls and other animal sounds, thunder and rain, waves upon a shore. All of these sounds can communicate something to us—when we listen.

As a speech and language pathologist with children and adults with disabilities such as autism, stroke, deafness, cerebral palsy, and emotional disturbance, I attempted using stories, music, and poetry to reach my clients. The more traditional methods of treatment were sometimes not nearly as effective. Then somewhere around 1979, I began offering to come into classrooms to provide what I called "language stimulation sessions" for all the children when I had the time. As all my children had special needs and, therefore, could use the language stimulation, the teachers welcomed the opportunity for this experience, which was very new for them. In fact, none of us was aware of this approach having been attempted at the time.

From there, I taught traditional dances that I had learned in Trinidad to stimulate sensory development and to expand the children's cultural awareness. The use of drum rhythms facilitated practice with recognizing and counting syllables. For articulation therapy, instead of using "nonsense syllables," so frequently referred to in speech pathology and audiology training programs, I found the use of words and syllables within actual but unfamiliar languages to be more functional and conceptually expansive for the children. We would then use these same words and phrases learned within a traditional story or would develop a new one as part of their auditory training. Because I had written stories, poetry, music, and plays for my kids to perform in the school assemblies, these efforts also contributed well to an increase in self-appreciation. Many of their teachers did not previously have the expectation that this kind of presentation by their children was possible; so, now, through the power of story, these children could receive their applause for a job well done, too.

## Chapter 13

# A Language of No Words

### Laura Simms

*Laura Simms has been traveling to Romania for the past six years, where she still carries on her storytelling work. She speaks here of going beyond translation as she comes to know a group of Roma (Gypsy) women, who, failing adequate translation, communicate in "a language of no words."*

What a year may not bring, an hour might.

—Roma proverb

The first day I met the Roma women it was the middle of a harsh Moldavian winter. We sat in an unheated room in a building in a city called Bacau. Leslie Hawke, the director of a remarkable project—taking women and children off the streets where they were begging, to give the mothers work and better living skills and send their children to classes to prepare for school—had asked if I would tell stories.

The women sat in a circle, huddled close for warmth. Their arms were tightly held against their bodies like the adolescents who confront me in high schools in Manhattan with suspicion. My translator was a therapist, Daniela Cornestean, whom I had worked with for two years in a more northern city. We had developed a magnificent dance of translation from the first summer of our project with teenagers in the peasant village of Malini, to our work with orphans in the city of Iasi. Daniela's English was excellent and her listening so immediate that she discovered a way to turn my sentences into Romanian without interrupting the flow of relationship between myself and listeners.

I decided to tell a story about my Grandma Ida and her telling me stories about growing up in the mud-thick town of Lomza in Poland when she was a child. The unspoken backdrop to her story was the sorrow of anti-Semitism that provoked her to travel at sixteen to America in 1900. I was aware of the racism against the gypsies. Before World War II they lived side by side with Jews in the cities where I now worked. I wondered if this connection was meaningful, as the mothers leaned forward to listen ever so slightly.

Daniela translated beneath my words like a musician. There were pauses. We had learned that the gestures, the feeling, the breath, the rhythm, the reception of events all need a certain intuitive timing and space to move back and forward between us and the audience: a triangle of attention.

At the start I was aware of Daniela's struggle to concentrate and my own short sentences to make certain we would fall into the tempo of communication that depended not only on us but the women in the circle. They never revealed any interest with their eyes. So, I avoided making eye contact. Yet, I could feel the shift in the air in the room and saw their strongly gripped arms loosen. The hard wall of mistrust melted somewhat as they made their way into the story that they imagined.

Perhaps it provided associations for them. Childhood, death, magic, mothers, food, old languages, gardens, and memories. The stuff of everyone's remembrances.

There were sentences I spoke mimicking Grandma Ida's Yiddish sing-song accent. I used Yiddish words. Daniela had to ask me what they meant. I translated for her. She translated for them. They laughed when I acted like my grandmother, bending my body ever so slightly, feeling the weight and age of her immigrant body that seemed always in another world; as if she were baked in Polish foods and sounds and memories. Her voice held an entire universe of languages. Ida spoke Yiddish and Polish. She also knew Russian, German, and French. She incanted a weird version of English that I adored and imitated when I was a child. There were so many stories she never told. The few details I had, now spun into the fabric of this story, were filled with a sense of something I could not grasp. I wondered if that yearning was fragrant in the sound of my voice. I had no way of knowing.

I asked about their own childhood memories. I asked for a description of a place they recalled. Those that chose to respond gave very curt answers. A few women turned away. Daniela repeated, "We had a garden in front of the house where my mother grew vegetables." "My grandmother lived in a wooden house. Her hair was black even when she was old." "The place I liked was a shed behind the house." "The kitchen was outdoors."

A woman signaled with her hand for me to come closer. I got up and kneeled before her. I watched her eyes. Daniela translated. "We went to a meadow in the summer. There were fires and lots of talking." The space between our words was alive. Just as I had watched the mothers speak to Daniela, they now all watched me listen to Daniela, watching the woman who described the wind in the trees and the sound of a horse neighing. A language of no words passed between us. I repeated what Daniela said to me in English out loud to render each image into sound. I was mapping their stories in space with my voice. They shook their heads. Eyes widened.

"What do you think?" I whispered to Daniela. She said, "They are enjoying themselves. Look at their feet." I saw their feet were extended, no longer hidden under the chairs. She was translating gestures. "I think there is trust," she added.

Then an older woman, harshly thin and unbearably sad, obviously once beautiful, whose hair was covered in a traditional Romanian red headscarf, uncrossed her arms, "My father told me stories." She gestured, one finger circling in the air. "I do not remember the stories. I remember the circle of white smoke in the dark room, smoke around his lips that warmed the space we sat in." Daniela asked her a question for clarification and then repeated this fragment of memory to me. I felt I had been let into a house of few details, longing as I longed for my grandmother's past. But she said that was all she remembered.

It was the way it was said. I heard more than the words but could never explain what I heard. The image of the man's lips, of the intimacy between father and daughter, of the white smoke in the dark. It was a tale of a time and a world that had passed for her. Perhaps for all time.

I was a rider on a three-legged horse going slowly, not sure of reaching a destination. In fact, I know that my strength lay in my not having a destination. Of accepting that I was a stranger. A preconceived expectation about what was a story and what did I want to know or hear would have meant that I sought something and was not willing to know them as they were. I was *Gadje* ("a white person"), who had no language and no knowledge. So my relationship birthed in the process of translation where the awkward spaces gave us presence in otherness; and a chance to slow down.

I revealed that I was also the granddaughter of a Romanian Jewish woman, the wife of a Grand Rabbi, like a duchess, who had died when I was six months old. I offered them my tenuous connection to their history. One woman had been to Dorohoi, the area of Mahlia's birth, "There is a Tsigan village nearby that had been Jewish." Another woman told me about a Jewish family where her father worked: "They lived on the street where we are now, before the war." She described a tiled wood heater in the living room.

What happened in the two hours of our meeting could have happened in a half hour if I spoke Romanian and were alone.

But, because of my ignorance and my dependence on translation, I was able to be present with them in a way that was deeper than the exact words that were being shared. The attempt to engage with each other was bigger. I could be honestly ignorant. The not knowing became a rich kind of knowing; the translation of silence and seeing into meeting.

As the women were getting up to leave, I asked if they liked the storytelling. A few of the women stayed. The others were racing in their thin boots back onto the snow-covered street to catch a train to Buhusi, twenty minutes away, where their families waited.

A large woman, wearing an oversized faded Michael Jackson T-shirt under her jacket, spoke. Daniela had to lean in to hear her words since it was only to me that she sent her answer. Daniela related, "I liked it because I forgot about my problems. I remembered that in my childhood I was happy." Our time together was about remembering that joy could be recalled. It was not lost, as they had feared. I responded in Romanian, "*Mult-somesc.* Thank you." My mispronunciation brought laughter from the group that was left.

"Will you come again?" asked a woman, surprising me in English. She was young and looked like a gypsy of my imagination.

"I hope so. If I can come back, what would you want to do?"

She answered in Romanian to one of the staff who were standing near her, who repeated it in Romanian to Daniela, who repeated her words to me, "We want to tell stories to our children. We want to remember our hearts. Our lives are very hard."

I asked if the women knew their own languages. "Most do not," said Narcissa. "Do you know Tsigan stories?" I asked. "No," she answered all in English. Then she told me that her grandmother had been a traditional Roma. She showed me her silver rings and a silver bracelet, handcrafted, and told me a story about her grandmother giving them to her because "I am a real gypsy."

I spent the next six months traveling back and forth to Bacau under an Open Society Grant to give storytelling workshops. I wanted to have Daniela translate, but it was not possible. The staff volunteered, but they did not repeat what they heard. They did not respect the women. It was obvious when it was not accurate or even close to what was being said. I learned to listen to the sounds of the mother's voices more deeply as if I could hear the words behind the words.

I discovered in those times how much of a story is never spoken and how true listening has as much to do with trust and taste as with the literal meaning of sentences.

On one of our last days, when my Romanian had improved, and the women and I looked forward to our time together, although we knew it would not provide heat in the winter or repair the roofs of their ramshackle houses, we returned to the question of their childhood memories. I asked again for descriptions of precious places. They began to tell me stories, long stories, about their lives. When it was over, the women who had denied being Roma, denied knowing their language, all conspired in a moment of inspiration to give me a gift. One woman stood up. She clapped her hands. The others stood behind her. She began to sing an old song in an old language. Keeping the beat with their beaten down shoes, the other women sang behind her. Their beauty was the beauty of being. No one in the room understood the meaning of the words and there was no need for translation.

A good person will find a treasure even in poverty. A fool will find no luck even with wealth.

—Roma proverb

*Chapter 14*

# Tellers Travel

*After a posting about this book was put on the storytellers' listserv STORYTELL, I received several fascinating notes from tellers who have been put in positions in which they had to delve into other languages for their telling. Some of these brief notes are included here, along with tips on telling simple stories from Ruth Stotter, and a travel narrative of Roslyn Bresnick-Perry's trip to Cuba. Wherever they go, tellers seem to find a way to communicate across language barriers.*

## NOT JUST A MATTER OF LANGUAGE
### by Regina Ress

*Regina Ress, a New York City teller, writes, "The crazy thing about all this telling in Spanish is . . . I don't speak it that well. I sound pretty good, but I am far from fluent. But there is obviously something else going on, as I was invited to go to Spain after being heard in Brazil, and then again to Tenerife after being heard in Madrid. So it is not just a matter of 'language.'" Here Ress shows that storytelling success is possible despite language barriers.*

Why try to leap across the language barrier and tell stories in a foreign language? Well, for me, it is great fun. I begin with that, because if it isn't fun, don't do it! A more serious reason, of course, is that language is a bridge to other people and cultures.

I have told stories in English with sprinklings of Spanish for many years. In addition, a few years ago I started telling stories totally in Spanish. I was traveling each year to a different Latin American country, meeting the people, learning the language, and absorbing as much as I could of the cultures. I was getting so much from my experiences that I wanted to give something back. What I have to give is storytelling.

At first thought, it would seem that storytelling would be a hard art to share because it is language dependent. But, of course, storytelling is not simply its linguistic component; it also includes body language, gesture, movement, expression . . . the whole range of the performer's craft. Beyond all this is the interest in and love of a people and their language we display when we try to speak their language, when we cross that bridge to them. Our audience is affirmed and mutual respect and interest are fostered. So it is not just a matter of "language."

On one of my trips to Peru, I visited and told stories in Spanish in three schools. One was in a school in Yucay, a very small town in what is called El Valle Sagrado, the Sacred Valley of the Inca, near Cuzco. Later that day, I was walking around the town, stepping over the drainage ditch in the middle of the dirt street, avoiding wandering cattle, when some children started pointing and shouting *"La señora con cuentos!"* Soon I was surrounded by children and adults, dogs, roosters, and a boy with his cow, and I found myself telling the stories again in the middle of the street. I was there for the better part of an hour. We blocked the whole street. As I stood there, a part of me was witnessing the scene: a blue-eyed Norteamericana sharing stories, laughter, and goodwill with the local folks in a small town in the Andes. Indeed, not just a matter of language!

I have a personal story I tell about visiting a group of indigenous people in Costa Rica after 9/11. They wanted to learn more about what had happened, and I was asked to bring photographs of New York City and of the attack. After an amazing adventure getting to them, which included wading through the river (no *puentes*/bridges!), I was introduced in Cabecar, their language, by the chief and then in Spanish by the woman who had brought me to them. I showed the photos and in Spanish described the rivers (*Rio Hudson, Rio Este*), the bridges (*Puente de Brooklyn, Puente de Jorge Washington*), and the skyscrapers, *los rascacielos*. I had many photos of *Las Torres Gemelas*, Twin Towers. And then I said the words, *"Entonces, las Torres se derumbaron"* ("Then the Towers collapsed"). We then went through the book of photos of the attack. You could have heard a pin drop.

I left the book and photos with the Cabecar. After I left, for several months they thought about and discussed what had happened and then performed a three-day healing ritual for New York City and the whole earth. So with some very simple Spanish and some photographs, I brought New York City to these people on a remote mountain in Central America, and through my telling the story of my trip there, I have brought their love back out to New York . . . and beyond. There may not be a physical bridge across the river to them, but our shared story bridges our worlds, affirming the connection of all of us on the earth.

I have also told stories in international storytelling festivals in Spanish and English (with Spanish introductions) in Rio de Janeiro, Madrid, and Tenerife. Although I was nervous about my Spanish proficiency, my listeners were more than accepting. They were delighted with my willingness to leave the safety of my own language and risk telling in theirs.

One great experience I had in telling in Spanish was in June 2004, at *La Flauta Magica*, a club in Madrid that has featured storyteller Ana Garcia Castellano for more than a decade. I was fortunate to be in Madrid to celebrate her tenth anniversary and was asked to be one of the tellers. I was relaxed enough to "code switch," go back and forth between English and Spanish, including interacting and even joking with the audience. As I was there a few months after the bombing of Atocha train station, I told a story of the indestructible nature of freedom. The club was packed with people who love storytelling, their city, and freedom. Through the storytelling, I, a New Yorker who had experienced firsthand the attack of September 11th, embraced those Madrileños and they embraced me.

Of course, we don't have to tell stories totally in another language. Simply adding key words and phrases from the original language adds color, flavor, culture, and excitement to the telling. I've been using Spanish in stories for years here in New York, but recently at a branch of the New York Public Library in the Bronx a family from Brazil was among the folks gathered. I decided to tell the one Brazilian story I know and asked them to help me tell it. I know *um pouco* ("a little bit of") Portuguese, and together we put the Portuguese into the story. What an affirmation! (They confided in me that most Americans they meet don't even know that the language of Brazil is Portuguese.) At the same time, the Spanish speakers in the audience were learning how Portuguese is similar to and different from Spanish. Everyone loved it.

I am deeply convinced that storytelling, while language based, need not be language bound. When done with goodwill and care (language is a treasure: as with all treasures, handle with care!), telling stories in their original language or the language of the audience is rewarding to both teller and listeners. It adds color and texture, affirms language and culture, opens the heart, and makes new friends. And, as an extra bonus, it is fun!

## TRAVELING WITH SIMPLE TALES:
## TIPS FOR CROSSING LANGUAGE BARRIERS
### by Ruth Stotter

*Ruth Stotter travels abroad often. She and her retired-lawyer hus-band have the time and enthusiasm to visit many corners of the world. And Ruth likes to share stories wherever she goes. I asked her for some tips on making contact with children in the many cultures she encounters.*

### Mini Language Lessons

When I am going to a non-English-speaking country, I find a student at the University of California in Berkeley to give me a two-hour lesson in that language. I bring a list of words that I want to know. This includes animal sounds. Dogs, for example, do not say "woof" or "arf" in many other countries. I like to tell string stories and so include a few words to help tell these tales. For example, with the words *spider, spinning a web, good!* and *lunch,* I can tell the Mosquito tale found in *The Story Vine* by Anne Pellowski (Macmillan, 1984).

I also include a few sentences for humor. For example, I like to say, "I am from the moon," when people ask where I am from.

### A Simple Puppet Play

I also learn a simple puppet show, bringing with me a hand puppet de-signed to look like a native of that country. Here is the text:

*Hello, My Name is Ruth!*

Puppet:   Hello. My name is [popular name in that county]. This is my friend Ruth. I am teaching her to speak [the local language]. Ruth, what is this? [Puppet points to my eye.]
Ruth:   Eye.
Puppet:   You have two eyes. Ruth, what is this? [Puppet points to my ear.]
Ruth:   Ear.
Puppet:   You have two ears. Ruth, what is this? [Puppet points to my foot.]
Ruth:   Foot.

Puppet: You have two feet. Ruth, what is this? [Puppet points to my
hand.]
Ruth: Hand.
Puppet: Ruth! You have only one hand! I have two! [Puppet claps his
hands happily.]

Puppet and Ruth both take a bow.

This little dialogue and the story mentioned below are simple to learn.
Together with the approximate five hundred words I have learned from my
student teacher, I find I have amassed surprisingly useful phrases to use in
conversation.

### Do Not Touch Baby

Another story I take on my travels is called "Do Not Touch Baby." As this
has repetitive language, it is easy to memorize. Each finger of the hand is
mentioned and the "baby" is placed in the palm. The child touches the
palm and is told, "I told you not to touch the baby!" Children love to hear
the tale repeated in other languages after they have heard it in their native
language. "I understand Japanese!" a French child told me after hearing
the tale told a second time in Japanese. This story can be found—translated
into Spanish, French, German, Russian, Czech, Hungarian, Polish, Japanese, and Chinese—in *The Family Storytelling Handbook* by Anne Pellowski (Macmillan, 1987).

> Do Not Touch Baby
> Point to center of palm. "Here is Baby."
> Point to thumb. "Mama says: 'Do not touch Baby!'"
> Point to first finger. "Papa says: 'Do not touch Baby!'"
> Point to second finger. "Grandpa says: 'Do not touch Baby!'"
> Point to third finger. "Grandma says: 'Do not touch Baby!'"
> Point to fourth finger. "Sister says: 'Do not touch Baby!'"
> "Now show me. Where is Baby?"
> Child points to palm.
> "Do not touch Baby!"

## *SARAP! SARAP!* YUMMY TALES WITH A TWIST OF TAGALOG
### by Dianne de Las Casas

*Dianne intersperses bits of Tagalog into her tales to please Filipino listeners or to entice English speakers into her culture. Here she gives tips on telling abroad and on incorporating words from other languages into your telling at home.*

Born in the Philippines, I am half Filipina and half Caucasian American (of Welsh descent). Growing up, I learned some Tagalog (the national native dialect of the Philippines) through osmosis from my mother but was never formally taught the language. I lived in the Philippines as a child but traveled all over the world in a military family. In 2004, I was welcomed back to the Philippines as a *Balikbayan*, a Filipina coming back home. I toured in the Philippines in 2006, presenting teacher workshops in Manila, on the island of Cebu, and on the island of Davao. Though everyone spoke English, I interspersed Tagalog in my presentations, which everyone appreciated. Here are some tips on telling in the native language of the country you are visiting:

- If you are not fluent in the language, travel with a translator. My translator was so helpful not only with pronunciation of words but also in explaining culture and customs.
- Consult with experts on pronunciations. While telling in the Philippines, I once made the mistake of mispronouncing a word, which changed the meaning completely. It made the word obscene! Talk about embarrassment. Lesson learned. Practice and polish, being sure you know the correct pronunciation.
- Don't be afraid to incorporate native words into your stories. As long as you "do your homework" and treat the language and culture with respect, your audiences will appreciate your efforts.
- When telling to an audience that speaks no English, try to incorporate native words and choose visual stories. Select stories that lend themselves to being understood through dramatic facial expressions, body movement, and props. I told to a group of children at *Museo Pambata* (the children's museum in Manila) who spoke only Visayan, another Filipino dialect. Though the children did not understand English, they were able to understand the context of the stories through my animated movement and use of simple props. They laughed in all the right places and even sang in English. Their teacher told me that because of my interactive telling, there was no language barrier.

When telling in the United States, using another language in your telling not only lends authenticity to your tale but also gives audiences a taste of the culture.

- When incorporating another language, follow the word or phrase with the English translation. For example, when I tell in Tagalog, I say, "*Maligayang Pagdating*! Welcome Home!"
- Sometimes, words do not need translation if they are accompanied with facial or body language. For example, "*Sarap! Sarap!*" is translated by rubbing my stomach and licking my lips. Can you guess what it means? *Sarap*! means "yummy" or "delicious."
- Another way to engage an audience is to encourage audience participation. Allowing your audience to chant a repeating refrain in another language is a great way to teach them new words.

> "*Isa* (clap, clap), *dalawa* (clap, clap), *tatlo* (clap, clap), *apat* (clap, clap). One, two, three, four—he ran out the front door.
> "*Lima* (clap, clap), *anim* (clap, clap), *pito* (clap, clap), *walo* (clap, clap). Five, six, seven, eight—he ran straight to the gate."

Telling to an international audience is very rewarding whether abroad or at home. Don't be intimidated by another language. Use it to your advantage and it will add a richness and texture to your tales. *Mabuting kapalaran sa iyo*! Good luck to you!

*Dianne has written some short children's stories using Tagalog word inserts. In the following sample from her picture book* Lola's Kitchen, *she combines Tagalog numbers with Filipino food names. This idea could be adopted for use with other languages, too.*

> *Pitong* parts of chicken we sautee, until they're brown
> Lola's *adobong manok* is the best in town!
>
> *Anim* cups of water for the *Sinigang* broth
> I wipe off the counter with a colorful dishcloth.
>
> *Limang* more minutes until the *siopao* dough is done
> I help Lola stuff them; this is so much fun!*

*From Dianne de Las Casas, *Lola's Kitchen*, unpublished, copyright 2006.

## GROWLING ACROSS LANGUAGE A SUCCESS
by Bob Kanegis

*New Mexico teller Bob Kanegis writes of an unusual translation technique!*

I told stories "on the fly," so to speak, when I had the good fortune to spend a night at a wilderness lodge deep in Denali National Park. The others in the lodge were Swiss tourists. One of my fellow guests who spoke English well agreed to translate. One of the stories I told was *The Man Who Entertained the Bears*, a Tlingit tale originally collected around 1898 in Kake, Alaska, where many years earlier I'd spent a few months doing commercial fishing with a crew of elders.

There comes a part in the story where the old silvertip grizzly speaks to the man who has invited the bears to his house for a feast. I do my best to give a dignified oration in bear grunts. I have to say that the Swiss tourists were a dignified but rather serious group. They were listening with attention but not much emotion until I got to that part of the story, and my translator had to make a quick transition from German to bear grunts. There was laughter all around, and it certainly changed the whole energy of the evening.

## MAKING FRIENDS THROUGH TELLING . . .
## EVEN ACROSS LANGUAGE BARRIERS
by Cathryn Fairlee

*Cathryn Fairlee writes of her pleasure listening and sharing tales in Guangxi, China.*

In January 2006 I traveled to the northern hills of Guangxi, China, to revisit a Dong family we had visited in 2003. In 2003 we were so far out on the tangle of bus routes that took us to this village, it was necessary to stay overnight. We found a new Dong hotel, built in the traditional three-story wood-log style with funds from the government to help encourage minority tourism. Young proprietor Yang had been awarded a scholarship to be schooled in Shanghai in business, where he picked up a reasonable amount of English. He was fluent in Chinese, his second language.

I naturally asked if he knew anyone who told traditional stories. He said his mother knows hundreds of stories. "Do you think she would tell me a story?" Sure. She was my husband's age, 67, but looked older and spoke less Chinese than I did. I called her *nai nai*, grandma. She was quietly amused that my husband and I wanted to hear her tell a story in a language we did not understand. (I don't think at that time she knew I speak some Chinese from studying a year in Taiwan). But she demurely sat down and with very few gestures, but a twinkle in her eyes, told for about ten minutes.

I was enthralled just to hear the music of the Dong language being spoken at length. It is related to the Tibetan language, not Han Chinese. Grandma got up, I thanked her in Chinese, and she smiled and went into the other room. Then Yang began to translate the story. Three sentences into the story, I whispered to my husband, "My gracious, it is Beauty and the Beast!" And it was. Not from Disney or any Western fairy tale book, just that worldwide archetype. The beast, of course, was a dragon.

That night I was able to talk to grandma again and grandpa, whose Chinese was more fluent. He was just fascinated at being able to speak to any foreigner and showed me a video of a traditional Dong festival, in which the Han Chinese are the villains, complete with gangster fedoras and dark glasses! Their grandkids gathered around; I told them a simple finger story in Chinese; and they responded with a story in Chinese, of which I will have to admit, I understood very little. Yang was not around to translate.

As we planned another trip to China for January 2006, we stumbled upon Yang's email address online. He did not have one in 2003, and other than sending him the photo of him and his family, we had not kept in touch. We emailed right away and made reservations for two days in January. When we arrived, it was bitterly cold and those exquisite green rice paddies were a grim brown. His hotel was traditional enough that the only heat was a portable cast iron wok-like hearth barely off the floor. It was filled with sand and had charcoal glowing hot in the center, around which everyone huddled at night. We found grandma and grandpa had moved to the city to live with another son who had heat! I could not blame them.

Yang said he had told his mother we were coming and she very fondly remembered us. I said I was sad not to see her again. He offered to ask her if she wanted to come visit while we were there. Yes! So on the cell phones that are much more pervasive in China than here, he called, and she said she would be on the next bus. I was delighted. Embarrassingly, we did not recognize her when she spotted us downtown, and we just smiled and walked away when she said hello in Chinese. She was dressed in a very traditional way, with a white cloth on her head, silver hoops in her ears, and indigo pants and top. She appeared to be one of many old ladies trying to sell us something. When we later saw her at Yang's house, I was very apologetic and we had a nice chat.

After dinner that night, Yang said he would be willing to translate if we wanted to hear more stories. Yes! Another guest, a young French student, grandma, grandpa, Yang, my husband, and I crowded around the glowing hearth to hear stories. Grandma and grandpa took off their shoes and put them dangerously near the coals. Grandma began to tell, and Yang had evidently thought about this, or his mother had suggested it, because he would stop her every couple of paragraphs to translate. It was much more effective than him trying to remember the details, and not as disruptive as I would have thought, as I still enjoyed hearing her voice telling in the original Dong.

Every once in a while Yang would stop and ask her something for clarification. Every so often he and I would confer about the correct English word. Her first story was of a poor boy who is kind to a serpent, which turns out to be the dragon king's daughter. A delightful fairy tale. Then she asked me for a story. I had Chinese stories in my head, but that seemed silly, so I asked her what kind of story she wanted and she said, an American story. OK. I told "Brer Rabbit and the Goober Peas" with a little song in it. Yang told me that in China the rabbit is considered clever, too. Our French friend had never heard anything like it. I was very visual and we all laughed.

Grandma told another story of Good Brother versus Bad Brother, which was hilariously scatological. Yang and I conferred on what the English word for "bad gas from bottom" was called, and I spelled out F . . . A . . . R . . . T in my palm. "Not good," he said. I agreed and everyone laughed. I told them the Gold Rush story of Charlie Parkhurst, a woman dressed as a man who drove stagecoach and was probably the first woman in the United States to vote for a president. I think they were more intrigued than entertained. They asked for another, and in honor of our student friend, I told the French medieval werewolf *lais*, "Garwuf." Everyone was most satisfied. I gave grandma an earring with a dancing fairy on it and had Yang explain that the story she told first was called in English a "fairy" tale. She was delighted and went over to the mirror and put it on with the traditional silver earring. We hugged as we said goodbye and that is my fondest memory of our three-week trip to the south of China.

---

## LET THE STORIES COME
### by Mary Grace Ketner

*Mary Grace Ketner tells of a remarkable experience when a Russian song learned as a child makes its way into her story . . . and a Russian listener fills in the blanks.*

When the Institute of Texan Cultures, where I work as an education specialist, hosted the exhibit "Children Just Like Me," I told stories from some of the cultures represented in the exhibit.

One day we had a drop-in visit of a group of hope-to-be parents and their hope-to-be adopted Russian children as well as some staff from the organizing adoptive agency and a translator, about thirty people in all, I'd say. This group experience is a step in the adoption process, and apparently it was a week or two of sessions and outings.

The parents were ecstatic at the portion of the exhibit that featured an 8-year-old Olia and her dancing class, and many, many photographs were taken of the children wearing tutus and trying on ballet slippers. When I discovered who they were, I talked with their translator about helping me tell the Russian story, "The Fool of the World and the Flying Ship," and she agreed.

What I didn't think to tell her—didn't even remember at first—was that I include the song "Otchi Chor-nya" ("Dark Eyes") in my telling. Now, I had learned that as a child from a songbook my mother had in which the Russian was written phonetically; I didn't even know whether I was pronouncing it correctly or remembering it correctly, but it had come back to me when I started working on that story. I have the fool of the world and his accumulating friends sing it each time they "sailed away, singing the old songs." When I tell it in schools, English-speaking students pick up on the phrases and join in. At the end I have the fool sing it—it's a love song—in English when he marries the princess, and children are enchanted by the meaning of the words they've learned. I especially enjoy getting to look into the dark eyes of our south Texas Mexican-American students and sing it to them.

So, we translated the story, me saying a sentence or two, then pausing for her to repeat—which she did with great natural verve! When I got to the first round of singing, I suddenly realized—uh-oh! Who do I think I am, anyway, singing this Russian song to Russians? But there was no going back, so I launched right in. This time, instead of waiting for me to pause and let her repeat, the translator joined right in with me! It turned out, those old phonetic spellings weren't so bad after all, and I'd remembered all but the last line, which was gibberish in my version. I couldn't pick up the correct words on the run, so in the subsequent "sailed-away-singing-the-old-songs," I simply gestured to her and she took over.

I treasure getting to be a part of those children and hopeful couples hearing the same story and singing together. Now, I don't always have that kind of boldness, but I'm very grateful that I did that day and also very appreciative of getting to meet such a gifted translator and story buddy!

## FOUND IN TRANSLATION
by Caren S. Neile

*Caren reports on her visit to the* Jornada Contarte *storytelling festival in Havana, Cuba, in 2004 in the company of the lively eighty-one years young Jewish teller, Roslyn Bresnick-Perry.*

Picture this: I am sitting with the nationally acclaimed, eighty-something storyteller Roslyn Bresnick-Perry, of cheerful disposition and grandma girth, at a wrought-iron table in the cool, dimly lit taste-testing lounge of a Havana rum factory. We are surrounded by two dozen or so young, boisterous tellers from Cuba, Peru, Colombia, Mexico, and other Hispanic countries, whom we have joined for a storytelling festival and conference. We have just spent five days with these charming, mainly non-English-speaking performers.

The most important part of the trip, for them at least, is now at hand. The festival awards ceremony, which can make or sidetrack a young career, is taking place on the balcony-cum-stage six feet above our heads.

Roslyn's Spanish vocabulary is nil, and mine makes me sound, on a good day, like an only slightly precocious toddler. So, during the brief speeches that precede and follow each award, we whisper. About our frustration at not knowing what people are saying. (Our translator has apparently decided the event is not worth our understanding.) About our disappointment that we're leaving Cuba the next day. About the contest itself.

"You know," Roslyn says, sipping at the rum and Coke we have each collected following the group tour of the factory. "I really don't believe in competition for storytelling. It's not appropriate to judge one teller over another. Everyone has something different to say and a different way to say it. Giving prizes is like comparing apples and . . . ."

In the midst of the jumble of Spanish, Roslyn suddenly catches the sound of her name. All eyes, and smiles, turn to her.

"What does it mean?" she asks me, a little breathless.

"It means," I say, "that you've won a prize."

❖   ❖   ❖

There is an old joke about a cat who stalks a bird by chirping at it. When at last he fools his prey into captivity, he happily observes, "It pays to learn a foreign language."

This joke comes to mind several times in the spring of 2004, as I prepare to travel to Havana for the conference/festival called Jornada Contarte. The invitation has been extended through a Cuban storyteller friend, and I am elated that my proposal on storytelling with senior citizens has been accepted for the conference. I also plan to participate in the festival, although I am more a teacher than a performer.

Although I have studied several languages and live in south Florida, where Spanish is practically *de rigueur*, or however you say that in Spanish, I have never gotten around to learning it. This trip, however, is a great incentive. I buy a couple of books—everything short of *Spanish for Dummies*—borrow language tapes and CDs, add the *telenovela* channels to my most-watched-list on satellite TV and a Spanish love song station to my car radio, appeal to the generosity of a former Berlitz-teacher friend, and *ahora!* I am a Spanish language student.

Not for a moment do I imagine that I will be able to perform a story or present a paper without a translator. I simply want to barter at the market. I plan to carry a gift to the friend of a friend and am looking forward to holding a conversation with him. Above all, I want to follow, more or less, the stories at the festival, and communicate, more or less, with my fellow participants.

*       *       *

Fast forward to a month or so before my trip. I am drinking coffee with my dear friend and mentor Roslyn. I casually mention my upcoming adventure ninety miles off the Florida coast.

Roslyn practically leaps from the couch. "Oh, take me with you!" she cries. "I've always wanted to see Cuba before I die! And besides, who better to teach about storytelling with seniors than a senior storyteller?"

She has a point, but I hesitate. "Um, how's your Spanish?"

"Rotten. It's pretty much impossible for me to learn a new language. I think it's partly my age, and partly my dyslexia." Her eyes light up. "But I'm fluent in Yiddish!"

Now, I dearly love Roslyn, and I greatly respect her as a storyteller. But I had planned to immerse myself in the language and the culture. If I travel with a friend, particularly someone who cannot learn a foreign language, I will have less opportunity to do so. I have a second, more queasy-making reservation, as well. I have long noted that Roz is eighty-one going on eight. Her repertoire even includes a story in which her cousin Dottie accuses her of always needing to be the center of attention. Was I denying the great Roslyn Bresnick-Perry the chance for a trip to Havana because I was afraid of a little social competition? Was I about to penalize Roz for my childhood relationship with a more interesting older sister? *Claro que no!* Storytelling in Havana with this super-lively, super-witty, super-sociable Jewish *abuela*? At the very least, I figured, I would get a good story out of it.

We quickly work out a way to co-present. And so the story begins.

*       *       *

We are introduced to our translator on the bus that stands waiting for us at the Havana airport. Miriam is in her late thirties, highly intelligent, attractive, and feisty. She and Roz bond in minutes. Miriam correctly recognizes that Roslyn requires her services a lot more than I do, and, besides, Roz is more fun. Already she is hooting in excitement at the billboards, which advertise not products, but politics. She is pointing to the aging cars and the listing buildings. Add to that the fact that healthy, hearty, huggable senior citizens are rare in Cuba, and RBP is an instant celebrity.

But I am not bitter. At least not yet. I have Spanish to learn. Who knows, maybe a translator would cramp my style! From the moment I unlock the door to my hotel room—as soon as the power returns after one of the city's habitual blackouts—I switch on CNN *en Español*. It plays every minute I am there, serving as the soundtrack even to my dreams.

*    *    *

That first night, the entire group, maybe twenty of us, are invited to the apartment of Elvia Peréz, the director of one of the city's two storytelling schools. Roslyn and I arrive with Miriam and Mirtha, a Cuban-American anthropologist in the group who is also staying in our hotel. We are offered popcorn, cold drinks, and something with burritos. Soon, everyone is sitting in a circle, on the floor, or in hard chairs scattered around the living room. Two young men come forward, one with a guitar. Together, they alternately tell and sing a story that, Miriam tells us, is fairly bawdy. The audience reels with laughter. Another teller comes forward and another. With each performance, we are told, the stories grow more and more risque.

I know Roslyn well enough to see the wheels turning behind her shining eyes. "I've got a story," she says at last to Miriam. "Will you translate for me?" Miriam, of course, is delighted.

"There's just one thing," Roz says. "Do you know the word *udder?*"

"Yes, sure. Other. *Otra.*"

"No, no, *udder.* Umm, teat. The part on a cow that you milk." Finally, in frustration, she makes the universal sign for milking: two fists, one rhythmically pulling down, while the other lifts up.

Miriam laughs. "Ah, yes, yes!"

They proceed to tell Roslyn's story. It is a delightful immigrant tale about the time her father, new to America, was in a shop and chanced upon a barrel of one his favorite foods: cow udders. Seeing no one behind the counter, he laid down some money. As there were no bags or newspaper with which to wrap his purchase, he stuffed an udder down the front of his pants. He then caught a subway home. He soon noticed two women staring at his pants in horror. He looked down to see that one of the teats had escaped through his open fly. No problem! He took out his penknife and cut it off. When the women gasped, he said, "Don't worry! I've got three more!"

As she tells the story, Roslyn's face colors. Her eyes flash; her gestures are broad. Miriam is laughing as she translates. And the storytellers! By the end of the story, they are fairly rolling on the floor. Roslyn is a brilliant success.

\*        \*        \*

In the days that follow, Miriam and Roslyn can usually be found walking together, their arms linked. This means that Miriam is not always there for me when I need her, particularly in the theater where most of the festival is taking place. It is difficult, if not impossible, for her to whisper translations to both of us.

But I am nothing if not a trooper. I sit in the darkened theater with a Spanish-English dictionary, trying to make out some of the words from the stories. What is *bruja*? Ah, witch. Comes in handy at a storytelling festival.

\*        \*        \*

It is time for our presentation on storytelling with seniors. We each have ten minutes to speak before questions are asked. First, I lecture on scholarly research on the psychological and emotional benefits of storytelling on the elderly brain. Miriam dutifully translates, the group respectfully listens, and I am pleased. I wrap up by describing several of the techniques I use to encourage storytelling.

Then it is Roz's turn. With passion and humor, she relates a few of her experiences with seniors. At the end of our talk, the audience members ask her several questions, while I sit quietly by, telling myself that after all, her piece *was* more interesting.

\*        \*        \*

Mirtha the anthropologist has a dear friend among the Cuban storytellers, a man named Jorge. Roslyn and I spend a fair amount of time with them both. One evening, Jorge shows us a restaurant that is good, cheap, and not for tourists. Mirtha and Jorge are rattling away in Spanish. I am trying to follow. Roz's eyes wander around the room.

I do not know what prompts her. I am pretty sure it is nothing at all, although it could have been the sound system, or a word she catches on the menu, or something in the conversation. Suddenly, she beings to hum *Guantanamera*. Just like that, in the middle of dinner in a quiet restaurant. In the midst of a conversation.

I have had enough. I turn to Mirtha and Jorge for support, but they are already joining her in the second verse. I sink down as far as I can in the banquette and helplessly finger my dictionary.

\*        \*        \*

Another afternoon listening to stories. How is it that nearly every one of them comes with a song, and nearly all the tellers know these songs? I discover that that they are folk songs, inserted into the stories to make them interactive.

All at once, I recognize a word. Then another. I look up a third. I know this story! It is *The Giving Tree*, by Shel Silverstein. Not one of my favorites, but at that moment, I am convinced it is a classic.

Now it is Roslyn's turn to perform. She and Miriam have carefully re-hearsed her story. Miriam makes a few suggestions on elements that might be clearer if done a little differently. The tale concerns Roslyn's *shtetl*, the tiny Jewish ghetto in Bellarusse, where she was born. It is clear from the audience reaction that Miriam perfectly catches the rhythms and nuances. The audience cheers for them both. Later, Roz mentions how strange it is to get a laugh a minute after she's made a joke.

*    *    *

Roslyn, Miriam, and I do a little sightseeing in Old Havana. We stop at a market, where I buy a multicolored mask. I am pleased that I can conduct the transaction by myself, but unsure about the colors. Later, when we are seated at a nearby outdoor café, I decide to exchange the mask for a green one, which will better match my living room. Miriam offers to help, but I think I can pull it off. I am thrilled that I can make myself understood, with a minimum of sign language, to the woman who has sold it to me. When I return to the table, we ask the waiter to take our picture. Roslyn and the translator have their arms around each other; I am off to the side.

*    *    *

Before leaving for Havana, a colleague had given me bars of soap and other gifts for a dear friend whom I promised to look up. My colleague spoke no Spanish; his friend no English, but their translated relationship had nonetheless been deep. I call the friend and manage to set up an appointment for him to meet me in the hotel lobby. Roslyn, who is curious to meet him, accompanies me.

The man arrives, smiling and grateful. We exchange pleasantries in Spanglish. Then we switch to Spanish. I don't know how it happens, but there it is. We are carrying on a conversation about the festival, about our mutual acquaintance, about Havana, about the gifts. Every once in a while, Roslyn asks a question, and grudgingly I translate. I look over at her. Her face has fallen; she is bored and annoyed. I cannot blame her; I am being terribly rude. But neither can I stop myself. I am actually having a conversa-tion in Spanish! My hard work has paid off! I am connecting with the Cuban people—*por fin*!

*    *    *

I begin to make small friendships among some of the young people in the group. One or two remember the colleague who told me about the trip in the first place. Another knows English quite well. A fourth is particularly interested in storytelling with the elderly, and I give her the book I have brought on the subject.

Roslyn cannot talk much to the young storytellers. Still, they surround her. They adopt her. When they sing, she la-las with them. When they dance, she joins in. When they walk through the streets or stand around waiting for a performance, she rests her arms on their shoulders or gives them hugs.

I am put in mind of something I learned as a beginning speaker: Audiences recall only seven percent of the content of your speech, but thirty-eight percent of the sound, and fifty-five percent of the visuals.

*     *     *

The elderly woman who half an hour before had disparaged storytelling contests jumps to her feet as her name is called. Jaunty guitar music begins to play, and she dances up the steps to the stage. Once there, she swivels her hips and waves her arms to the beat. Her performance continues for a minute or two, to the immense pleasure of the crowd below. Then she accepts the "storytellers' choice" award, judged by the participants themselves. Along with the certificate, she receives a bouquet of flowers.

Roslyn's cheeks are pink, her eyes moist. "Thank you," she tells the crowd in English, her voice soft with emotion. "I have never been so honored in my life." She calls up Miriam to the stage and hands her the bouquet.

*     *     *

Two years later, the certificate, which Roslyn had laminated on her return, hangs at the entranceway to her office. It is a testament to the power of language for a woman who despaired of learning one. Whenever I visit her, I read it, in Spanish.

And I learn.

*Chapter 15*

# On the Translator's Art

*Margaret Read MacDonald*

Most storytelling translation happens on the spot. A translator is provided . . . or met briefly before the performance . . . and the translator just does the best possible to reproduce the story in another language. Sometimes the teller and the translator are able to work together at length before the performance. In these cases phrases can be chosen that replicate not only the meaning . . . but also the rhythm and flow of the original tale. When Paula Martín and I were working on her translation of my *Parent's Guide to Storytelling*, we spent a lot of time emailing translation possibilities back and forth between Seattle and Argentina. In many cases we opted for a rhythmic Spanish choice that kept up the playful nature of the tale, rather than a literal word-for-word translation. Paula had translated me in performance on several occasions and knew exactly how the tale should play onstage.

Though the writer's translation attempts are somewhat different from those of the speaking translator, I think some comments from the literary translator's concerns might help us think about the oral translating we do as well.

Ibrahim Muhawi has written about the difficulties of translating the spoken folktale into printed text for his book *Speak Bird, Speak Again* (Indiana University Press, 1989).

> Folktale style, though oral, is not spontaneous, like conversation: nor is it improvised, like personal narratives. . . . Folktale orality is highly mannered, replete with grammatical, rhetorical, and narrative patterns of all sorts.[*]

*From "On Translating Palestinian Folk Tales: Comparative Stylistics and the Semiotics of Genre" in *Arabic Grammar and Linguistics* (Curzon, 1999), p. 342.

Because of these stylistic elements, a faithful translation cannot just give the sense of the tale. Something of the style must also be conveyed.

Robert Wechsler cites several translators in his interesting book *Performing Without a Stage: The Art of Literary Translation.*†

> . . . to be a translator is to suppress your own voice in favor of another's, to spend your time worrying over the other's problems, manipulating the other's images and characters, expressing the other's vision and ideas. (p. 32)

The translator must choose not only what in the original to preserve and what to give up, but also what to add. All the elements I've been talking about—rhythm, sound, vision, humor, effect, syntax, familiarity vs. foreignness, ease vs. difficulty, ambiguity vs. clarity, meaning vs. form— not only have to be dealt with, but they have to be balanced against each other, one preserved, the other lost, two given up to keep one that is more important in the particular context (Wechsler, p. 139).

### On Dialect:

To the original-language reader, dialect gives a concrete impression of place and class. But dialect has meaning only in its language. The translator is placed in a difficult dilemma: does he use a recognizable English-language dialect that is roughly equivalent (say, Appalachian for Slovak mountain folk), or does he try to create something that suggests the original but does not exist in English? Gregory Rabassa opts for the latter solution:

> 'People try to take, say, a class dialect from Spanish and put it into a class dialect in English, and it doesn't work, because you made that person into an English speaker, and that's not it. What I would do with, say, a gaucho, is not to try to make him into a cowboy. Make him into an English-speaking gaucho. You've got to invent. It has to sound like English, but also sound like a gaucho. There are ways.' (Wechsler, p.136)

### On Humor:

Humor is about getting it. It's usually not a matter of bringing subtle signs over into another language, but of creating the same combination of laughter and understanding. So what does a translator do when face to face with humor? Well, the first thing he should do is forget the idea of running and hiding behind literal translation; it just won't cut the mustard. He has to be exceptionally creative, to transform the humor into something that works just as well in English and that conveys pretty much the same idea (Wechsler, p.135).

---

†Selections from Robert Wechsler, *Performing Without a Stage: The Art of Literary Translation.* (North Haven, CT.: Catbird Press, 1998), reprinted here with permission of Robert Wechsler and Catbird Press.

**The Fidelity Required of a Translator:**
They have different sorts of obligations to different sorts of things: the original work which is trying to find new life in a new language, the language and literary culture in which the original work was written, the literary culture the translator grew up with and works in and cannot get away from, and the handicapped audience for his work, which is especially needy and which the translator's publisher cares about more than anything else. Translation is not about betrayal, but rather about the balancing of, the impossible attempt to fulfill, a variety of often contradictory obligations. A responsible translator will always fall short, but will never be unfaithful (Wechsler, p. 113).

Wechsler quotes the Argentinean writer Jorge Luis Borges, in his high praise of the translator's art: "The translator's work is more subtle, more civilized than that of the writer: the translator clearly comes after the writer. Translation is a more advanced stage of civilization" (p. 9).

Perhaps the translator's highest reward is that of pleasing the originator of the first text . . . author or teller. Eliot Weinberger said of his translations for his friend Octavio Paz:

> At the last reading we did, at the Metropolitan Museum, Paz was saying — we were talking about my translations — and he was quoting Valéry, who said when he read the Spanish translations of his own poems, "I just love myself in Spanish." And Octavio said, "You know when I read my poems in English, I just love myself in English."

And perhaps closest to our own plight is Neruda's comment on the translation of poetry:

> Perhaps the real "original" behind any translation occurs not in the written poem, but in the poet's voice speaking the verse aloud . . . a translator may also pick up vocal tones, intensities, rhythms, and pauses that will reveal how the poet heard a word, a phrase, a line, a passage . . . what translating comes down to is listening — listening now to what the poet's voice said, now to one's own voice as it finds what to say.*

With the useful advice in this book, perhaps we can all match our translations to our tellers so well that they too will exclaim . . . "I just LOVE myself in Japanese!" Or Spanish . . . or German . . . or . . . .

---

*John Felstiner, *Translating Neruda: The Way to Macchu Picchu* (Stanford, CA: Stanford University Press, 1980), p. 151.

# Chapter 16

# Bibliography

Here are citations for some bilingual folktales from authors contributing to this book and a few other tellers. We also include certain collections that appeared originally in English and are now available in other languages. Hopefully some of these will serve as shortcuts in your efforts to prepare tales in other languages.

## BILINGUAL FOLKTALES

### Japanese

Fujita, Hiroko. *Ohanashi Obasan no Kodogu* (Auntie Storyteller's useful toys). Tokyo: Isseisha, 1996, pp. 4–6. This handbook for beginning tellers in Japan was adapted by Fran Stallings into *Stories to Play With: Kids' Tales Told with Puppets, Paper, Toys, and Imagination*. Little Rock: August House, 1999.

Fujita, Hiroko, and Fran Stallings. *Furan-san to Hiroko no Ohanashi no Hon* (Fran & Hiroko's story book) #1. Tokyo: Isseisha, 1999. ISBN 4–87077-154–3 printed in Japanese (stories, notes, front and back matter) with English (stories only) on facing pages. English CD, stories only, now called *Traveling Tales #1*. Available from Fran Stallings.

———. *Furan-san to Hiroko no Ohanashi no Hon* (Fran & Hiroko's story book) #2. Tokyo: Isseisha, 1999. ISBN 4–87077-157–8 printed in Japanese (stories, notes, front and back matter) with English (stories only) on facing pages. English CD, stories only, now called *Traveling Tales #2*. Available from Fran Stallings.

———. *Ohanashi Obasan no Sekai no Ohanashi Mukashimukashi* (Auntie Storyteller's world tales of long ago). Tokyo: Isseisha, 2001. Japanese with English translations inserted as pamphlet. info@isseisha.net; http://www.isseisha.net

## Spanish

Cruz, Alejandro. Adapted by Rosalma Zubizarreta-Ada. *The Woman Who Outshone the Sun: The Legend of Lucia Zenteno/ La mujer que brillaba mas aun que el sol: la leyenda de Lucia Zenteno*. Illus. Francisco Olivera. Children's Book Press, 1991.

González, Lucía M.. *The Bossy Gallito/ El gallo de bodas: A Traditional Cuban Folktale*. Illus. Lulu Delacre. Scholastic, 1994.

Hayes, Joe. Joe is author of numerous bilingual picture books and collections, including these:

———. *El Cucyu: A Bogeyman Cuento in English and Spanish* . Illus. Honorio Robledo. Cinco Puntos Press, 2001.

———. *The Day It Snowed Tortillas: El dia que nevo tortillas* . Illus. Antonio Castro Lopez. Cinco Puntos Press, 2003.

———. *A Spoon for Every Bite: Una Cuchara Para Cada Bocada*. Illus. Rebecca Leer. Cinco Puntos Press, 2005.

———. *Tell Me a Cuento: Cuéntame un Story*. Illus. Geronimo Garcia. Cinco Puntos Press, 1998. *National Public Radio commentator Baxter Black, letter July 7, 1998:* "Thanks for the new version of Cuéntame un Story. . . . My five-year-old son has a stack of Spanish kids' story books taller than Pancho Villa's statue in Tucson Park. I have spoken only Spanish to him since his birth. . . . However, the single most useful "aid" to his learning to speak Spanish is and was *Tell Me a Cuento*. He listened to the tapes, both sides alternately, over and over, and I have read *El Terrible Tragadabas* so many times it is as imprinted in my brain as the stewardesses instructions on Aero Mosca. I think you could replace the entire U.S. bilingual education program, including the State Department crash course and Univision, with an annual new release of *Tell Me a Cuento* and we'd be world leaders again. It is so good, I'm not sure y'all really understand what you've got."

Loya, Olga. *Momentos Mágicos*: Magic Moments. August House, 1997. Fifteen Latin American tales from the storyteller Olga Loya. In both English and Spanish.

MacDonald, Margaret Read. *Conejito: A Folktale from Panama*. Illus. Geraldo Valério. August House, 2006. Incorporates Spanish words, repeated throughout the story. The singing refrain is provided in both English and Spanish.

———.*Cuentos que Van y Vienen: Comó inventar nuevos & narrar los favoritos de siempre*. Trans. Paula Martín. Buenos Aires: Aique, 2001. This is a translation of *A Parent's Guide to Storytelling* (August House, 2001). The English text is in the rear of the book. http://www.aique.com.ar/

Pérez, Elvia. *From the Winds of Manguito: Cuban Folktales in English and Spanish/ Desde los vientos de Manguito: Cuentos folkórico de Cuba, en ingles y español*. Trans. Paula Martín. Ed. Margaret Read MacDonald. Libraries Unlimited, 2004. Folktales and cante-fables from the Habana teller, Elvia Pérez.

Vigil, Angel. *The Corn Woman: Stories and Legends of the Hispanic Southwest/ La*

*Mujer del Maiz: Cuentos y Leyendos de Sudoest Hispanica.* Libraries Unlimited, 1994. Forty-five folktales, fifteen of which are presented also in Spanish. An audiotape with Angel telling tales from this book in both Spanish and English is available.

## Thai

MacDonald, Margaret Read. *The Girl Who Wore Too Much: A Folktale from Thailand.* Thai text by Supaporn Vathanaprida. Illus. Yvonne LeBrun Davis. August House, 1998.

## ENGLISH FOLKTALES TRANSLATED INTO OTHER LANGUAGES

### Finnish

Wolkstein, Diane. *The Magic Orange Tree and Other Haitian Folktales.* Salainen Kirjasto.
MacDonald, Margaret Read. *Kana, tipu ja kitara.* Helsinki: Vau'kirija, 2007. [Finnish trans. of *A Hen, a Chick, and a String Guitar* by Margaret Read MacDonald, Barefoot Books, 2005.]

### French

MacDonald, Margaret Read. *Choisi la Paix: 33 Contes et Proverbes des 4 Coins du Monde* (Peace tales: world folktales to talk about). Illus. Dominique Künli-Leclerc. Trans. Rajni Chopra. GRAD, 2003.
———. *Soignons notre Terre: 41 contes et proverbes de 4 coins du monde* (Earth care: World folktales to talk about). Illus. Anne Presse-Faure. Trans. Emmanuelle Chauvet. GRAD, 2005.
GRAD France, 228 Rue du Manet, 74130 Bonneville, France; grad.fr@grad-france. org; http://www.grad-france.org/

### Indonesian (Bahasa Indonesia)

MacDonald, Margaret. *Cerita-Cerita Perdamaian: Cerita Rakyat dari Berbagai Penjuru Dunia* (Peace tales: world folktales to talk about). Illus. Bamban Shakuntala. Trans. Rosalia Emmy Lestari. Penerbit Kanisius, 2004.
———. *Cerita-Cerita Pelestarian Lingkungan: Cerita Rakyat Dari Berbagai Penjuru Dunia* (Earth care: world folktales to talk about). Illus. Bambang Shakuntala. Trans. Florentina Christi Wardani. Penerbit Kanisius, 2004.
Penerbit Kanisius, Jl. Cempaka 9, Dereson, Yogyakarta, 55281, Indonesia; office@ kanisiusmedia.com

## Japanese

MacDonald, Margaret Read. *Kattate Ageteyo! Kodomotachini-Ohanashi No Katari-kata Gaidobukk* (A parent's guide to storytelling). Trans. Ryoko Sato. Tokyo: Amu Shobu, 2002. kuni@amushobo.com; http://www.amushobo.com/

———. *Akari Ga Kieta Sono* (When the lights go out). Illus. Iku Dekune. Trans. Ryoko Sato. Tokyo: Amu Shobu, 2004. kuni@amushobo.com; http://www.amushobo.com/

———. *Sanpunkan de Katareru Ohanashi* (Three minute tales). Illus. Iku Dekune. Trans. Ryoko Sato. Amu Shobu, 2005. kuni@amushobo.com; http://www.amushobo.com/

———. *Storytelling Nyumon* (The storyteller's start-up book). Trans. Masako Sueyoshi and Yukari Sueyoshi. Tokyo: Isseisha, 2006.

Smith, Jimmy Neil. *Homespun. Storyteller–tachi gendai America no folklore.* Trans. Shugi Ahiko. Tokyo: Taishukan Publishing Co., LTD, 1992.

Spagnoli, Cathy. *Uguisu Hime; Two Tell Tales.* Kanazawa, Japan: 2006. Bilingual (Japanese-English) Storytelling CD.

Sueyoshi, Masako, and Margaret Read MacDonald. *Motto Ohanashi to Asobou* (Let's play some more). Tokyo: Isseisha, 2005. Includes Japanese translations of "Jack and the Robbers" and others. info@isseisha.net; http://www.isseisha.net

Wolkstein, Dianne. *Mahou no orenji no ki.* (The magic orange tree and other Haitian folktales). Trans. Masako Shimizu. Tokyo: Iwanami Shoten Publishing, 1984.

## Korean

Forest, Heather. *Wisdom Tales from Around the World.* Seoul: Haneon, 2006.

———. *Wonder Tales from Around the World.* Seoul: Haneon, 2006.

MacDonald, Margaret Read. *Maumi Pyung-Hwaul Junun Joun Yiyakee* (Peace tales: world folktales to talk about). Seoul: Haneon, 2004. haneon@haneon.com; http://www.haneon.com

———. *The Squeaky Door.* Illus. Mary Newell DePalma. Gipun, 2006.

———. *Tok Tok Han Mabela* (Mabela the clever). Illus. Tim Coffey. Trans. Hae Suk Um. Montessori Korea Co., Ltd., 2003.

Spagnoli, Cathy. *Il(n)yeone Aho(p)mari, Eohung Eohung; Nine-in-One, Grr!Grr!* Seoul: Chekgori, 2004.

———. *Asia Jeonraedongwhaui Storytelling.* Treasury of Asian Stories and Activities. Daejeon: Hannam, 2007.

## Malay

Spagnoli, Cathy. *Sehari Dalam Hidup Priya; Priya's Day.* Kuala Lumpur: Malaysian Book Centre, 2006. (Bahasa Melayu-English)

## Tamil

Spagnoli, Cathy. *Priyavin Oru Naal; Priya's Day*. Kuala Lumpur: Malaysian Book
     Centre, 2006. (Tamil-English). Also from Chennai: Tulika.
*Priya's Day* is also available from Tulika Publishers in Hindi, Malayalam, and Kan-
     nada.
Chennai: Tulika, 1998.

## OTHERS

The British publisher Mantralingua offers nicely illustrated picture books
in many bilingual editions. The tellings are not especially "tellable," but it
does have a small selection of fables and folktales in its series. The range
of languages is impressive: Albanian, Arabic, Bengali, Chinese, Croatian,
Farsi, French, German, Gujarati, Hindi, Italian, Panjabi, Polish, Portuguese, Somali, Spanish, Tamil, Turkish, Urdu, and Vietnamese. http://
www.mantralingua.com/media.php?media=book

# Index

# About the Editor
# and the Contributors

**Mama Edie Armstrong** has provided speech therapy services for over thirty years. Her storytelling profession grew from her efforts to reach multiply challenged populations. Blending the two now allows her to meet the challenges of presenting to many diversified populations. 773-768-6773; MamaEdie2@aol.com

**Murti Bunanta** is the founder and president of Kelompok Pencinta Bacaan Anak (Society for the Advancement of Children's Literature), established in 1987. She is also president of the Indonesian Section of the International Board on Books for Youth (IBBY). She is the initiator of Motorbike Libraries to serve children in urban villages, remote areas, and devastated areas. Dr. Bunanta has published thirty-one folktale picture books for children. Her aim is to provide the children of Indonesia with a beautifully illustrated picture book from each of their provinces. Dr. Bunanta lectures at the University of Indonesia and abroad on children's literature and storytelling. Murti Bunanta is author of *Indonesian Folktales* (Libraries Unlimited, 2003). Kompleks Permata Hijau Block A/20, Jakarta 12210, Indonesia. murtib@cbn.net.id

**Kevin Cordi** is a nationally known storyteller and teacher who has told in twenty-five states, England, and Japan. He believes stories keep us connected and help us experience diversity. He is currently working on a Ph.D. at Ohio State University on "narrative telling and dramatic inquiry." He is the "first full-time high school storytelling teacher in the country." He can be reached at kctells@youthstorytelling.com or his website at http://www.youthstorytelling.com.

**Livia de Almeida** is a journalist and editor of *Veja Rio*, a weekly magazine, for which she writes on art, children's entertainment, and food. She is a member of the Mil e Umas storytelling troupe and has organized Tellabration and other storytelling events in Rio de Janeiro. Livia has toured the

United States twice and was a featured performer, along with Roberto Carlos Ramos, at the King County Library System StoryFest International. Livia compiled the Aesop award–winning collection *Brazilian Folktales* (Libraries Unlimited, 2006). Rua Bulhões de Carvalho 33/404, 22080-000, Rio de Janeiro, Brazil. liviafrombr@gmail.com

**Dianne de Las Casas** is an author and award-winning storyteller who tours internationally presenting programs, teacher training, workshops, and artist residencies. Her performances, dubbed "traditional folklore gone fun," are full of energetic audience participation. Her multi-award-winning CDs include *Jambalaya—Stories with Louisiana Flavor, World Fiesta—Celebrations in Story and Song,* and *Jump, Jiggle & Jam—A Rhythmic Romp Through Story Land.* Dianne's books include *The Story Biz Handbook; Story Fest: Crafting Story Theater Scripts; Kamishibai Story Theater: The Art of Picture Telling;* and *Handmade Tales: Stories to Make and Take.* Visit her website at http://www.storyconnection.net and subscribe to Story Connection Express, an educational e-zine for parents and teachers. dianne@ storyconnection.net; storyconnection@gmail.com

**Martin Ellrodt**, tells stories in German, English, and Spanish. His favorites come from oral tradition, but there's a great love for world literature such as Shakespeare and Cervantes, too. Besides his storytelling around the world, he's also organizing festivals and started the first storytelling center in Germany three years ago. martin@ellrodt.de; http://www.ellrodt.de

**Cathryn Fairlee** is a fifth-generation Californian who grew up in foggy redwood country and went forth to travel the world. She performed in theater while working as a junior high school librarian. This combination naturally brewed into storytelling. Currently she is working on her Master's degree in History and has been a full-time teller since 1999. Still traveling the world, she enjoys tasting and serving up myths and folktales wherever she finds herself. 4699 Grove St., Healdsburg, CA 95448; 707-433-2297; cfair@ monitor.net; http://www.sonic.net/~cfair

**Hiroko Fujita** tells traditional country tales she learned from elders and farmers during her childhood in mountainous rural Fukushima Prefecture, Japan. Formerly a preschool teacher and primary grade librarian, she now visits Japanese schools and libraries where her storytelling keeps the old tales and games alive for the cell phone generation. She also speaks to older students and parents' groups about the importance of the old stories in preserving cultural roots, reinforcing bonds between generations, and laying groundwork for literacy. Fujita-san and Fran Stallings have toured the United States eleven times. In 2003 they received the National Storytelling

Network's "International Story-Bridge" award for their work on both sides of the Pacific. Fujita-san lives in Kashiwa City just east of Tokyo. Fujita-san's tales are available in *Folktales from the Japanese Countryside*, as told by Hiroko Fujita, edited by Fran Stalling (Libraries Unlimited, 2007).

**Ben Haggarty** has been pioneering professional storytelling in Britain since 1981 both as a performer and as an organizer of major festivals and events. He's performed in international festivals in twenty-three countries and has researched the epic singing traditions of Central Asia, Turkey, and Central India. Since 2001 he has been the official storyteller with Yo Yo Ma's Silk Road Ensemble and in 2007 was appointed an honorary professor of storytelling at the University of Berlin. epicstory@aol.com; http://www.crickcrackclub.com

**Michael Harvey** is one of the United Kingdom's leading contemporary storytellers. He works at major international festivals in Britain, Europe, and North America telling traditional stories from the Celtic countries and beyond and was commissioned to perform a contemporary retelling of *Culhwch and Olwen*, the oldest extant Arthurian story, to celebrate the tenth anniversary of Beyond the Border International Storytelling Festival. Michael has appeared frequently on television and radio and works with dancers, musicians, visual artists, and many major cultural institutions as well as performers from Brazil, India, and Europe. He tells in Welsh, English, and French. michael@michaelharvey.org; http://www.michaelharvey.org

**Joe Hayes** is an award-winning author and storyteller—a nationally recognized teller of tales from the Hispanic, Native American, and Anglo cultures. As a child, Joe lived in a small town in southern Arizona. From his schoolmates and friends, many of whom were Mexican-American, he began to learn Spanish. When his own children were young, Joe enjoyed telling them stories. He then began looking for other children to share stories with. It seemed natural to him to use both Spanish and English when telling his stories to children. Joe has worked full time as a storyteller since 1979. His pioneering work in bilingual Spanish/English storytelling has earned him a distinctive place among the storytellers of the United States. joehayes@newmexico.com

**Priscilla Howe** began telling stories in her job as a children's librarian before becoming a full-time storyteller in 1993. A native New Englander, she lives in Lawrence, Kansas, and travels around the country and to Europe telling (almost) true stories, world folktales, and stories from books—all served with a generous dollop of humor. priscilla@priscillahowe.com; http://www.priscillahowe.com

**Jill Johnson** has spent almost half her working life overseas. As a young woman, she worked in Army Service Clubs in Korea and Vietnam. Later she joined the Peace Corps and spent six years in the Philippines working as a volunteer, teacher, editor, and performer. In the 1980s, she joined a volunteer medical relief team in northern Thailand assisting Laotian and Cambodian refugees. Ten years later, she spent two and a half years in Cameroon/Central West Africa, working with Peace Corps, Save the Children, and the United Nations Development Program as a training project director. Between 1993 and 1996, she worked in Morocco, Haiti, the Solomon Islands, and the Central African Republic as a training consultant. In 1997, Jill began telling in Jonesborough, Tennessee—calling storytelling "my sixth career." Those international experiences form the core of her storytelling. From her home on Whidbey Island in Washington State, Jill is still traveling—now as a performer and workshop facilitator. "Storytelling builds community; a sense of connection between people—it's joyous work!" 6439 Plum Tree Lane, Clinton, WA 98236; 360-341-2063; http://story@whidbey.com; http://www.seattlestorytelling.com

**Bob Kanegis** is the director of Future WAVE (Working for Alternatives to Violence Through Entertainment) and the founder of Tales & Trails Community Storytelling. He encourages others to tell their stories through initiatives such as The Endangered Stories Act and FEAST—Families Feasting and Storytelling Together. Tales & Trails; 254 Camino de la Tierra, Corrales, NM 87048. bob@storyconnection.com

**Lois Sprengnether Keel** shares these thoughts about herself: My original training and field was theater and that's my undergraduate degree. I started working as a librarian in 1970, while working on my Master's in Library Science, which I received in 1975. I also began storytelling in 1970. My interest in American Sign Language started as one of my two daughters has a hearing impairment. We began learning sign language as a form of enrichment for her. At one point she expected that everybody signed. It grew into a larger interest as her hearing declined. Today she hopes to use her ability to sign and an undergraduate degree in Psychology to work with special needs families. For my own part I began using sign language with storytelling and in church to maintain my skills, introduce the hearing to signing, and assist others in seeing as well as hearing what is said or sung. My other daughter had a son this past spring and I'm hoping he will learn to sign as he learns to speak. 5640 Farley Road, Clarkston, MI 48346. loissez@earthlink.net; http://www.LoiS-sez.com; http://www.michiganhumanities.org/touring/2006_2009/storyteller/index.htm

**Mary Grace Ketner** is an active storyteller in San Antonio, Texas, co-founder of the San Antonio Storytellers Association, and a museum educator at University of Texas at San Antonio's Institute of Texan Cultures

(ITC). She is the producer of two storytelling recordings for ITC: *Many Tricksters: Trickster Tales from Around the World*, and *YIKES! Scary Stories from the Texas Folklife Festival*, each being an olio of tales as told by several beloved Texas storytellers, including herself! She is the author of *Ganzy Remembers* (Atheneum, 1991). San Antonio, Texas, USA. mgteller@yahoo .com; http://www.talesandlegends.net

**Julia Klein,** born in southern Germany in 1971, works as a storyteller and educator. After graduating from Drama School in Ulm in 1995, she moved to Bremen. As a storyteller she performs in public and private spaces, indoors and outdoors, wherever people gather to hear stories. She also writes stories herself for both children and adults, and gives workshops on the use of storytelling in education. Graf Moltke Str. 35, 28211 Bremen; phone 0049-421-3467222; juliaklein2002@yahoo.de; http://www.geschich tenhaendlerin.de

**Angela Lloyd** earned her M.F.A. in Acting at the Florida State/Asolo Conservatory for Professional Actor Training. The daughter of a composer and engineer, her early childhood training was a crossroad of rhythm, music, poetry, and story. A musician and performing artist, she plays Autoharp, tenor guitar, spoon, and bell, and is an absolute *virtuosa* on her washboard. Her performances are based on an eclectic listener's ear; a personal inquiry through world stories and songs; and poetry that shines its single light for the journey. This appreciation for what was so naturally given in her early years has been the basis for her residencies in various states, culminating most recently in 2000–2007 as the storyteller in residence at the Walden School in Pasadena, California. Her annual storytelling projects have supported the school's mission, educational program, and curriculum for preschool through sixth-grade students. Angela marks her twentieth storytelling season in 2006–2007, as she continues to tour her performances and tutorials to regional (the touring and workshop roster for the Los Angeles Music Center Education Division) and national venues for performances, theater, and education. Go to http://www.angelalloyd.com for information regarding her award-winning recordings *Dreams and Other Realities* and *Sandburg Out Loud* and touring calendar. 10 Kemper Campbell Ranch Rd, #4; Victorville, CA 92395; phone 760-955-1321; fax: 760-951-8300; storyboat @aol.com

**Olga Loya** is a nationally known Latina storyteller, performance artist, teacher, and author who dramatically mixes Spanish and English in performances for adults, children, and families. Her repertoire demonstrates how diversity embraces the richness of cultures in the commonality and individuality of lives. Olga also performs a large selection of colorful tales from around the world that not only entertains but also expand audience awareness of other cultures. She has been a featured teller at the National Storytelling Festival as well as appearing at the Ghost Tales in 2001. P.O. Box 6482, San Jose, Ca 9550l; 408-448-4098; oloya1@mindspring.com

**Margaret Read MacDonald**, compiler of this book, is author of over fifty books on folklore and storytelling topics. MacDonald travels internationally, offering her "playing with story" workshops and performing for schools, libraries, and festivals, both alone and with musician Richard Scholtz. For information on her books, performances, and touring calendar, visit http://www.margaretreadmacdonald.com; 11507 NE 104th St., Kirkland, WA 98033; 425-827-6430; mrm@margaretreadmacdonald.com

**Paula Martín** is a storyteller, teacher, and writer from Buenos Aires, Argentina. She performs in English, in Spanish, and in both languages combined, and she has translated live performances of English-speaking storytellers in Argentina and in Cuba. As part of the duo *Sembrando Cuentos* (Sowing Stories), she has traveled in Argentina, the United States, Great Britain, Cuba, and Brazil. She translated Margaret Read MacDonald's book *A Parent"s Guide to Storytelling* into Spanish (*Cuentos Que Van y Vienen*, Aique Editorial) and Elvia Pèrez's book *From the Winds of Manguito/ Desde los vientos de Manguito* into English. Arismendi 2666 Ciudad de Buenos Aires, C1427DLF; phone 54114521-5983; paumar@fibertel.com.ar; http://www.sembrando-cuentos.com.ar

**Caren S. Neile**, M.F.A., Ph.D., is founding director of the South Florida Storytelling Project at Florida Atlantic University, where she teaches storytelling. Dr. Neile serves on the boards of the National Storytelling Network Healing Story Alliance and the Florida Storytelling Association. She is the founder of the Palm Beach County Storytelling Guild and managing editor of *Storytelling, Self, Society: An Interdisciplinary Journal of Storytelling Studies*. Dr. Neile has presented and performed throughout the United States, in Canada, and in the Caribbean. Her publications include *Hidden* (University of Wisconsin Press, 2002) and chapters in *A Beginner's Guide to Storytelling* (National Storytelling Press, 2003), *The Storytelling Classroom* (Teachers Ideas Press, 2006), and *Elie Wiesel and the Art of Storytelling* (2006). She is a 2005 recipient of a National Storytelling Network Oracle award for Regional Service and Leadership and has been featured on National Public Radio and in *Cosmopolitan* magazine. Director, South Florida Storytelling Project, Florida Atlantic University School of Communication and Multimedia Studies; 777 Glades Road, Boca Raton, Florida 33431-0991; 561-297-0042; carenina@bellsouth.net

**Maren Ostergaard** has been a children's librarian with the King County Library System for over ten years, where she has functioned as the Early Literacy/Outreach Librarian since January 2005. She earned a B.S. in Biology and a M.L.S. from the University of Washington. In addition, she continues to learn by raising her own children who are ages three, six, and ten. Maren Ostergaard, Early Literacy/Outreach Librarian; KCLS Service Center, 960 Newport Way, Issaquah, WA 98027; 425-369-3323; 1-877-905-2009 ext. 3323; fax 425–369-3204; ostergar@kcls.org

**Neppe Pettersson** is a full-time storyteller from Finland. She has been telling stories in television since 1989 and touring for live audiences for more than ten years in Finland, Scandinavia, and Europe. Neppe works with traditional stories for all ages and also gives workshops in storytelling. Neppe received the 2007 Vuoden Sadonkertoja "Storyteller of the Year" Award in Finland. Rådhusgatan 36 bostad 17; FI – 65100 Vasa, Finland; phone +358-50-358 6690; neppe@neppe.fi; http://www.neppe.fi

**Ricardo Provencio** is a counseling and storytelling faculty member at South Mountain Community College in Phoenix, Arizona. Ricardo tells ancient Mexican, Aztec, Mayan, and Spanish myths, legends, and folktales as well as personal, historical stories from his Latino, Mexican, and Southwestern historical and cultural roots and experiences. Ricardo has performed as a storyteller at the Jonesborough, Tennessee, National Storytelling Festival on the Regional Showcase stage, and been a featured teller at the Malibu by the Sea Festival; Nebraska Moonshell Festival; Maple Woods Community College Storytelling Festival; and Salina, Kansas, Smoky Hill River Festival. He has also performed at many Phoenix area elementary schools, libraries, museums, book fairs, educational organizations, conferences, and local community fiestas and events. ricardo.provencio@smcmail.maricopa.edu

**Kat Redniss** is currently completing her Masters degree in Educational Theatre and English at New York University's Steinhardt School of Education. She hopes to teach high school English, incorporating dramatic techniques in the classroom. Eventually she would like to pursue further study focusing on community-based literacy and interactive methods of increasing literacy. She holds a B.A. in English and Economics from Smith College. kar338@nyu.edu; kredniss@optonline.net

**Regina Ress**, award-winning storyteller, educator, and writer, has been performing and teaching for over thirty-five years from Broadway to Brazil. She has told stories in English and Spanish in a wide variety of settings in the United States, Latin America, and Europe, from grade schools to senior centers, from homeless shelters and prisons to Lincoln Center and the White House. Performances range from delightful folktales to some of the world's great mythologies including Aztec, Mayan, and Egyptian. She also tells original stories about New York City, love, and a life well lived. Regina teaches a graduate course on storytelling for New York University's program in Educational Theatre. She is grateful to be working in story. storyteller RRess@aol.com; http://www.storynet.org/directory

**Tim Sheppard** is much beloved by the storytelling community for his informative Storytelling FAQ. 4 Oakenhill Road, Brislington, Bristol, B54 4LR ENGLAND; phone 0117 977 6354; story@timsheppard.co.uk; http://www.timsheppard.co.uk/story

**Laura Simms** is an internationally acclaimed storyteller, author, educator, and activist who combines her knowledge of traditional myth and fairytale with true-life stories. Laura has been telling stories and teaching for over thirty years. She is a longtime advocate for compassionate action and human rights. She directs a community initiative to save a zoo in Romania, has developed a storytelling mentor program via the Internet, and maintains a highly respected storytelling residency. Her work can be viewed on http://www.laurasimms.com and http://www.lionsroar.us. She lives in New York City with her adopted son.

**Cathy Spagnoli** has given storytelling programs and workshops to thousands of listeners throughout Asia and the United States since 1986. Cathy has researched Asian storytelling traditions for three decades, with support from the Japan Foundation, the Korea Foundation, the Indian Ministry of Culture, the United States Information Agency, the U.S. State Department, and others. Cathy has written sixteen books on Asian tales and storytelling techniques. Her stories are also on several cassette tapes and CDs, and her storytelling articles have been published in numerous journals, anthologies, and in several encyclopedias. She and her husband, Indian sculptor Paramasivam, live on Vashon Island, Washington, and in Cholamandal Artists' Village in South India. Find out more about Cathy's programs and resources at http://www.cathyspagnoli.com; contact Cathy at cathy.spagnoli@gmail.com

**Fran Stallings** grew up in a storytelling family. She has worked as a professional storyteller since 1978, telling traditional tales and original creations nationwide and overseas. Fran has toured Japan five times with Fujita-san; they were featured at the 2005 Asian Congress of Storytellers in Singapore. Based in Bartlesville, Oklahoma, she has produced three CDs, published stories and articles, and edited books and magazines. For more tales by Frank and Fujita-san see *Folktales from the Japanese Countryside*, as told by Hiroko Fujita, edited by Fran Stalling (Libraries Unlimited, 2007). 1406 Macklyn Lane, Bartlesville, OK 74006-5419; 918-333-7390; http://www.franstallings.com

**Ruth Stotter** is former director of the Dominican University Storytelling program. She is the author of *About Story*; *More About Story*; and *The Golden Axe*. Ruth received the Reading the World Award from the University of San Francisco (2004) and is currently the consultant on storytelling for Puppeteers of America. In April 2006 she organized the first United States Gathering of String Enthusiasts. r.stotter@comcast.net

**Masako Sueyoshi** is on the board of directors of the Japan Storytelling Network and is a director and teacher of the Storytelling Seminar produced by the Japan Storytellers Association. Masako organizes Tellabration in Japan each November, and was organizer for the 2006 Japan Storytellers Association Conference. She has been a featured teller at festivals in the United States, Australia, Canada, Japan, Singapore, and at the National Storytelling Festival in Jonesborough, Tennessee. She is author of *Ohanashi to Asobo* (*Let's Play with Stories*), Isseisha, 2001; *Motto Ohanashi to Asobo*, Isseisha, 2005; *Mukashi Banashi World e Yokoso*, Isseisha, 2005; and translator, with Yukari Sueyoshi, of *Storytelling Nyumon* (*Storyteller's Start-up Book*) by Margaret Read MacDonald, Isseisha, 2006. 2-9-17 Yukarigaoka Sakura City, Chiba, 285-0858, JAPAN; phone and fax 81-43-462-7347; Onihime-yumegatari@nifty.com

**David Titus**, with a thread of a story and a piece of yarn, has traveled on six continents telling stories and teaching and collecting string figures. okteller@juno.com; http://www.Storyteller-Wordsmith.com; www.String FigureStore.com; http://www.StringMinistries.org

**Wajuppa Tossa** is an associate professor of English and American Literature at Mahasarakham University, Thailand. She received her Ph.D. in English and American Literature from Drew University. Dr. Tossa tours and gives storytelling performances in and outside of Thailand (Malaysia, Laos, Singapore, Hong Kong, China, Australia, The Netherlands, and the United States). She is particularly keen on the use of folktales and storytelling in her career as a teacher and facilitator of workshops. Her publications include *Phadaeng Nang Ai: A Translation of a Thai/Isan Folk Epic in Verse* and *Phya Khankhaak, the Toad King: A Translation of an Isan Fertility Myth in Verse* (Bucknell University Press, 1996); and "Engendering Cultural Pride Through Storytelling" in *The Arts, Education, and Social Change*, Lesley University Series in Arts and Education, vol. 9 (Peter Lang Publishing, 2005) and *Lao Folktales*, with Kongdevane Nettavong (Libraries Unlimited, 2008). 48 Mu 14 Wang Sarakham, Tambon Koeng, Amphoe

Muang, Mahasarakham 44000, Thailand; phone 66 43 742 443; wajuppa @yahoo.com

**Karee Wardrop**, CSC, M.A., has been a nationally certified interpreter/ translator since 1986, working between English and American Sign Language. She has degrees in Interpreting, Theatre Arts, and Dance and continues to study education and creative writing. As a freelance interpreter, she has been fortunate to work in a wide variety of situations, spanning the continuum of possibilities from the intimacy of one-on-one family situations to the formality of large-scale national conferences; from grade school playgrounds to Shakespeare productions. In each and every situation, the responsibility of carrying another's communication is great, and the assisting in the successful connection between individuals is thrilling. Karee lives with her family in Bellingham, Washington. kareew@earthlink.net

**Jen and Nat Whitman** have been working for over a decade as international educators and professional storytellers. They are committed to exploring the role of storytelling in teaching culturally and linguistically diverse students. The Whitman Story Sampler performs as a tandem storytelling team in libraries, schools, and festivals worldwide. They also offer workshops for teachers on the varied uses of storytelling in the classroom. (The Whitmans are finishing a tour in Hong Kong and will be based in Bonn, Germany 2007–2009). U.S. contact: 11507 NE 104th St., Kirkland, Washington 98033; 425-827-6430; jenmacwhitman@yahoo.com; whitmantellers @gmail.com; http://www.margaretreadmacdonald.com/index.cfm?fuseaction= Friends.Whitman

**Judith Wynhausen** is of the "baby boomer generation" and has been involved in music, acting, and teaching for most of her life. It was only natural that she would become a storyteller. She began telling stories in 1992 and tells in both English and Spanish. She earned degrees in Music Education and Theatre, and also completed training as a Waldorf kindergarten teacher. She is mother to four children and many animals. In addition to storytelling, Judith loves to dance and plays with an African marimba ensemble. 2202 E. 47th St., Joplin, Missouri 64804; phone: 417-782-6983; judith@judithtells.com ; http://www.judithtells.com